FEEL THROUGH ME

JOHN WHITMEYER

ISBN 978-1-64569-963-7 (paperback)
ISBN 978-1-64569-964-4 (digital)

Christian Faith Publishing, Inc.
832 Park Avenue
Meadville, PA 16335
www.christianfaithpublishing.com

Printed in the United States of America

CHAPTER 1

THEN THE GROUND MOVED BELOW ME

"WAIT UNTIL YOU HEAR what the psychic said!" Erin exclaimed breathlessly as she rushed in the back door, setting her shopping bags down on the kitchen table.

"Hi, doll," I said, reaching out to help with her coat. My wife, Erin, and her friends had scheduled a reading with a local medium that afternoon, and she seemed anxious to share her experience.

"She was actually kind of annoying at first. She kept talking about throat surgery for you!" Erin said, rolling her eyes. "She must have said it like five times! I had to ask her if we could move on!"

I laughed. I knew Erin well, and when she was feeling impatient, she would let you know.

"Hold out your hand!" she suddenly demanded. I playfully obeyed, revealing my right palm, face up on top of hers. She studied it carefully, running her index finger across the lines. After seventeen years of marriage, Erin was fully aware that I was not much of a believer in psychics or bad omens. I took this moment to admire her pretty face as she focused more intently on the palm of my hand. Her warm touch was meaningful, as always.

"Well?" I prodded, amused. "What else did she say?" She furrowed her brows a bit, a little habit she had whenever she was concentrating or confused. She smiled knowingly and with a nod looked up at me with conviction.

"Yup, I'm going to die before you," she stated matter-of-factly. I laughed and rolled my eyes.

"Yeah, okay!" I scoffed, flashing the okay sign with my other hand. I hadn't laughed in a while, but considering the state of my health at that time, the idea of Erin leaving this world before me sounded downright ludicrous.

"Well, that's what she said," Erin retorted and dropped my hand. "She said I would see it in your palm, and she was right. It's all there, just like she described."

I could only pull her close and kiss her. "Well, I guess we'd better get some lovin' in now while we can!" I suggested.

"Stop making fun of me! I'm serious!" She laughingly pushed me away. I stopped joking and looked at her tenderly.

"I'm not making fun of you, doll. I love you." I smiled and gave her a firm hug, then rubbed her back slowly. She was my girl. There was no way I was letting her leave this world before me.

Erin and I had taken our vows long ago. In that uniting moment, we held hands and offered ourselves to each other in special ways with powerful obligations. Although we promised "till death do us part," we never imagined the parting.

More than a year earlier, I had been diagnosed with a rare debilitating muscle disease that had stripped me of the ability to accomplish the simplest of daily tasks. There were times I struggled to dress myself or even walk. Due to the ferocious onset of the disease and its rarity, I had come frighteningly close to death as my doctors raced to come up with a diagnosis and treatment.

This past year had been very stressful on both of us, and our relationship had certainly been tested mainly due to the impact of my health crisis, financial and otherwise. Our lives were changed, seemingly in an instant. The irony of the psychic's premonition was not lost on me.

Uncertainty lingered in the air that night; my mind grew thick, and I found it difficult to sleep. I kept thinking about what the psychic had said about the throat surgery. Last year I had a procedure performed on my throat while in the hospital as part of my diagnosis. Was the psychic actually picking up on my death instead? That would certainly make more sense. Erin was the picture of health and vitality. A fearful voice inside me kept whispering that something was going to go terribly wrong, and I couldn't do a damn thing to stop it. Till death do us part?

No way! I have to live!

One afternoon a couple of weeks later, Erin returned home after a tennis match, exuberant and bubbling over about all the great shots she got in. It had been quite a while since I had seen her so happy and upbeat, and I sat back, soaking in every bit of the entertaining scene that was playing out before me. Erin in her form-fitting, short, white tennis skirt and matching white sneakers stood with her racket in hand demonstrating her athletic prowess.

"You should have seen it! You wouldn't have believed it! I had my weight back like you always tell me. I was positioned perfectly and *wham!*" she said, exaggerating her swing. "I smashed it to the other corner! She didn't stand a chance!" I grinned and jumped for my glass on the table. She almost smashed that too.

I had played tennis with Erin on many occasions, and I knew what that looked like. She was amazingly gifted in many ways, but she was no athlete. She continued with her theatrical demonstration, ignoring me, reenacting her winning shots with untempered enthusiasm.

I couldn't remember the last time I had seen Erin this carefree and joyful. She was always a bright light, but in moments like these— moments of pure happiness—she beamed even brighter, and I loved her even more.

We had planned a quiet evening with friends that night. It had been quite some time since we entertained. It was something we had always enjoyed but had been unable to do with my recovery progressing so slowly.

"It's chilly. Maybe we should have a fire? What do you think?" Erin asked, rubbing her hands together. February evenings in New England were notoriously bitter.

"Great idea! I'll grab some wood," I called out, picking up my coat. I was feeling strong enough to take on this simple task, and it felt good to contribute to the evening's preparations.

"Be careful!" Erin called after me. "It was a bit icy out there today! Maybe throw some salt down so no one has a slip and fall."

"Okay!" I replied, stepping out into the brisk night air. A nice, relaxing evening by a crackling fire seemed the perfect thing.

Our guests, Pat and his wife, Cheryl, soon arrived. We had been close friends with them for about ten years, and our girls were best friends with their daughter Emma. This evening, their kids stayed home, and our daughter Brittany and son Johnny were watching a movie upstairs, having eaten their favorite McDonalds dinner earlier. Our other daughter Kylie was sleeping at a friend's house.

We settled down with our guests in the family room, sitting in front of the warm glow of the fire. Erin poured everyone a glass of wine.

"John, how have you been feeling?" Pat leaned forward, concerned. "You look good!"

"Oh, I'm hanging in there," I replied awkwardly. I knew Pat deserved a more honest answer but didn't want to dampen everyone's spirits.

"He's doing a bit better than he was. That's for sure!" Erin chimed in, patting my knee. "This new treatment finally seems to be helping." She smiled knowingly at me, not missing a beat. "So, Cheryl, tell me! What's been going on with you? What have you been up to?" Erin gracefully steered the conversation away from me, and I was extremely grateful. She knew I hated feeling like a spectacle, even though our friends were well-meaning.

The evening flowed nicely with lively conversation, laughter, and good wine. When dinner was ready, we moved to the dining room where Erin had set a lovely table with fresh-cut flowers adorning the center. When we were all seated, Erin lifted her glass to our guests.

"Cheers! Thank you for coming, guys. We are so happy you are here. It's been too long!" she said, flashing her familiar wink.

"Thank you for having us," Pat replied, lifting his glass. "It has been too long. We are just so happy to see you both doing well. Cheers!" Erin smiled warmly at us over the successive sound of clinking glasses.

Letting those close to her know she cared about them was a priority for Erin, and she had a way of making people feel appreciated. It was one of her many natural gifts. I watched her from across the table, just taking it all in—her flushed cheeks, sparkling blue eyes with that little hint of mischief, her girlish smile. I felt a wave of gratitude for being able to share my life with her. Radiating happiness, Erin looked amazingly youthful, like the girl I fell in love with back in college. For a moment, I quietly basked in her light.

The pleasant evening ended fairly early, and our friends prepared to leave.

"Yeah, we sure can't hang like we used to!" Pat joked, pulling on his coat.

"Tell me about it!" I laughed.

"Speak for yourselves!" Erin exclaimed. "You guys are boring! Cheryl and I are going out dancing!" We all cracked up. Erin was well known among our friends for her fun-loving side.

"Be careful on those steps!" I called out to them as they stepped out into the night and closed the door behind them.

After our guests left, Erin and I sat in front of the fire and relaxed for a bit. Brittany came down from her room and joined us. Although my stamina had improved recently, this evening had taken a lot out of me. The warmth of the fire and the soft couch were comforting, and I struggled to keep my eyes open as I drifted in and out of a light sleep. Erin surprised me with a gentle nudge of her elbow and said, "You look tired. Why don't you go up to bed?" I thought about it for a bit.

"I think I will," I finally replied, slowly rising to my feet. Erin watched to see if I was going to need assistance, now an automatic response. This was a sobering reminder that our life as we had known it previously had changed.

"Good night, guys," I said softly as I walked out of the room.

"Good night," Erin and Brittany called back.

I felt a twinge of inadequacy as I slowly made my way upstairs. In earlier days, I would have gone to bed after Erin as my mind and body were once too active to settle down for the night easily.

I nestled into our bed, wrapping myself in the cool sheets and warm comforter. I closed my eyes as I felt my sore muscles relax, relishing the peaceful moments of a rewarding evening. As I drifted off to sleep, I felt a sense of contentment and a renewed yet cautious glimmer of hope. I knew Erin and I were strong enough to face any challenge together.

As sweet dreams can move heaven and earth, through the depths of my sleep I felt the ground move below me, two distinct tremors to be exact.

Awakened abruptly and confused as to why, I looked over to find Erin lying in bed next to me and was surprised by the strange look on her face. She was lying on her back, her body rigid, seemingly locked in place. She was staring, unblinking, over her right shoulder. Her arms were crisscrossed, the right forearm lying atop the left with her hands clenched tightly into fists.

"Erin? What's wrong?" I asked softly. When she didn't respond, I struggled to pull myself up onto my knees on the mattress alongside her. Something was very wrong. I kneeled next to her, grabbed her right hand, and tried to straighten out her arm to pull her toward me. Her arm did not move. I tried repeatedly to straighten it and failed because she was locked so tightly.

"Erin!" I called out again, tapping her cheeks lightly. Nothing, not a blink, not a twitch. Nothing.

I managed to slide off the bed and get myself to a standing position. With effort, I pulled her across the bed by her feet and was able to position her along the end.

"Erin, can you hear me? Erin?"

Panic began to set in. There was still no response.

Is she breathing? I couldn't readily tell. I remembered Erin carried an inhaler in her purse for occasional bouts with asthma, although she rarely needed it. My weakness and lack of mobility took a momentary back seat as adrenaline propelled me down the stairs. I headed straight for her purse and grabbed her inhaler. Now out of breath myself, I quickly returned to her.

My God, how much time has gone by? How long has she not been breathing? I took a deep inhale of her asthma medication, and I gave the exhale to Erin mouth to mouth, desperately trying to resuscitate her. I quickly repeated this same step two more times. The third time it occurred to me that the air was flowing freely between us. The air was getting to her lungs which meant her airway was open.

Then why isn't she breathing? Feeling dizzy from the medication, I struggled to recover my own breath. Frantically I reached for the phone next to the bed. As I dialed 911, I continued crying out, "Erin!"

"This is 911. What's your emergency?" the dispatcher asked in a monotone voice.

"Please send help fast! It's my wife! She's not breathing!" I said frantically before shouting out my address. "Please hurry, please!"

"Help is on the way," she advised. "Where is your wife now?"

"She's lying across the end of the bed," I replied helplessly. Each second that ticked by was a matter of life or death. I knew this.

"Move your wife to the floor," she instructed firmly. I panicked.

"I can't! I'm not strong enough. I'll drop her!" I pleaded.

"Okay, keep her where she is," the dispatcher said, her tone even. "You need to begin chest compressions. Do you know where to place your hands?" She confirmed their placement on Erin's chest. "Start counting one, two, three," she instructed, sounding confident in my ability. "Do this until you get to thirty." Following the dispatcher's lead, my hands pressed rhythmically up and down, compressing Erin's breastbone.

"Am I going to hurt her? This feels like I am pressing too hard!" I asked, worried. I just wanted her to breathe. "Why isn't she breathing?" I shouted as my desperation grew. "Are they coming? Is someone coming?" I pleaded.

"Yes. They are on their way. They will be arriving shortly," the dispatcher reassured in a calming voice. "Just keep doing the chest compressions until they get there."

After another thirty compressions, there was still no change.

"Erin, can you hear me?" I screamed louder. I could feel her slipping away from me. The dispatcher reminded me not to stop and to do another thirty compressions. Just as I began another set, the doorbell rang downstairs.

Thank God! Finally!

"Someone is here!" I exclaimed to the dispatcher. "I have to let them in!"

"Go let them in," she advised. I didn't want to leave Erin, but I had no choice.

I turned and staggered as quickly as I could back down the stairs and swung open the door. The first police officer had arrived, and his imposing frame filled the doorway.

"She's this way. Follow me!" I gestured, heading quickly toward the stairs. With an oxygen tank in hand, the officer quickly followed me upstairs to where Erin was still lying motionless.

"Do you know what happened?" the officer asked, automatically resuming chest compressions.

"I don't know. I was sleeping. She just stopped breathing," I replied, struggling to put shorts on my wife who hadn't planned on company when she went to bed.

Within seconds, officers two, three, and four had arrived and found their way to our bedroom on their own. I paced back and forth, grasping at my hair with my shaking hands. This had to be a bad dream. Unfortunately, the scene was much too real to deny.

Several more police officers arrived as well as EMTs, and they quickly moved Erin to the floor and surrounded her. She remained unresponsive.

I backed slowly away as the room swelled with first responders. Our bedroom, our most intimate, peaceful space had come alive. Just moments before, Erin and I had been sleeping there soundly, and now it was bustling with bright lights and strangers. As the unfathomable scene played out before me, I felt as if I was drifting up out of my body, watching all the kinetic activity from some distant place.

As priceless seconds ticked by, my bleary eyes scanned the room. I noticed the officers' uniforms with their colorful sewn-in patches displayed like street signs that told the story of their credentials. The EMT tackle boxes, an elongated oxygen tank, breathing tubes, and guns that now occupied our bedroom told me these unfamiliar faces came well prepared.

I had to look away from it all, and my eyes stopped on our wedding picture proudly displayed above our bed. Our youthful smiles so full of hope for the future offered no indication that this moment was looming ahead of us.

I drifted helplessly around the perimeter of the room, numb. Erin was just *lying* there, unmoving, not responding.

"Has she taken any drugs? Is she on any medications?" an EMT called to me.

"No, she isn't taking anything," I defensively snapped back.

What was he implying? They continued working on her. I could see them preparing to use a defibrillator.

"Clear!" someone shouted, and a split second later, I saw Erin's body bounce from the floor. Another second passed.

"Nothing. Let's try it again."

"Clear!" The medic pressed pads to Erin's chest, and her body jumped again.

I had to look away, and to my horror, I saw my thirteen-year-old daughter, Brittany, looking on from the hallway.

"Please stay in your room," I begged her.

"Is Mom going to be okay?" she asked, pressing for an answer.

"They are doing everything they can," I tried to sound reassuring. "Please just go back in your room."

Brittany must have sensed the seriousness of the situation because she pressed no further and walked back into her room. Moments later, I heard her terrified scream. I wanted to run to her, but I was bound to the nightmare that was playing out before me.

Activity swirled up and down the stairs like a tornado. The clanking of equipment, the staticky, muffled sounds of the officers' radios, loud footsteps on the stairs, the hushed official tones of officers' conversations outside the bedroom—all replaced the once-peaceful quiet of the night. None of it seemed real. The numbness was spreading within me.

As the moments passed by, conversation turned to mindless chitchat among those of us not working on Erin. Small talk. As strangely out of place as it seemed, the sound of it kept me from crumbling. The seconds continued to tick by, unrelenting.

My God. Johnny is sleeping in his room. Is he hearing any of this? Could he really be sleeping through all this chaos?

"We are transporting her to the hospital," an officer was talking to me. "Do you have someone who can come stay with the kids?"

"Yes, I can call someone," I responded numbly.

Our friend Pat, who had just been laughing with us over dinner a few hours earlier, seemed the best choice. I didn't remember dialing the phone.

"Pat, it's John. There's trouble with Erin. She is going to the hospital, and we need someone to watch the kids for us." I heard myself say to him over the sound of the EMTs still working frantically to revive my wife.

"I'll be right over."

I was told I should follow the ambulance to the hospital. As I stood in the kitchen absently looking for my keys, I could hear the heavy clanking sounds of the gurney as the EMTs brought Erin down the stairs. I couldn't bring myself to look as they headed for the front door.

This can't be happening. This is not happening. This is not happening. Life as I had known it was slipping away and being replaced with an utter nightmare.

The cold darkness enveloped me as I walked outside and opened my frozen car door. As I slid into the driver's seat and closed it behind me, an awful thought flitted through my mind. I just closed the door to the life I knew. Pushing the dark thought away, I inserted the key into the ignition and listened as the engine haltingly started. I sat there staring at my frozen breath as it formed icy clouds in the air, stunned.

What the hell just happened?

I peered through my rearview mirror at the six police cars, fire truck, and ambulance all parked in front of our house. I watched their spinning lights reflecting off the snow and our neighbor's houses in a dazzling yet horrifying light show that illuminated the entire neighborhood.

In case I wanted to forget.

I knew Erin was a minute or two ahead of me as I backed out of the driveway, and I began to feel very alone. In the darkest depths of my soul, I knew what I was driving myself to face, and I couldn't do it alone.

On my way to the hospital, I remembered our friend Dea lived just down the road. She was one of Erin's best friends and a nurse practitioner with a lot of connections at the hospital. It was after two in the morning, but I knew Dea could offer some much needed support, and I found myself pulling in to her driveway. I frantically knocked on the door and rang the doorbell over and over. She finally opened the door in her robe, sleepy eyes squinting to focus on me.

"My God, John, what's going on?"

"It's Erin, Dea. She's gone to the hospital, and it's not good. Something happened tonight. I don't know what, but please come with me," I rambled.

She was dressed in about thirty seconds. We both hurried to the car, and I screeched out of the driveway. With each moment that passed, Erin seemed farther away from me.

"John, what happened?" Dea asked again.

"I don't know!" I replied. "One minute she was sleeping, then she wasn't breathing! She wasn't responding to anything we did, and they've taken her to the hospital!" Dea frowned in the dark. She looked worried.

We sat in silence as I sped through the night, closing the distance between us and Erin. A cold terror began to grow within me as I thought about what awaited me.

Ten minutes felt like forever, and we finally arrived. The nurse at the front desk saw us approaching and pressed the button to open the doors. They swung open with excruciating slowness. I pushed past them and hurried over to the reception desk.

"Is my wife okay?" I pleaded. "Is Erin okay?"

The receptionist remained expressionless as she stood up and began walking out from behind the desk.

"I don't have any information, but you can follow me," she replied. She wordlessly ushered us into a small, empty waiting room. There were a few chairs along the wall, and as we sat down, the faint glimmer of hope I had been clinging to began to dwindle. "Someone will be in shortly," the woman said quietly as she left the room and closed the door.

Dea suddenly sprang to life. The shock of being awakened in the middle of the night with news that her best friend's life was in danger had worn off, and she strode out of the room muttering something about finding out what was going on. I could hear her outside the room talking in a raised voice, presumably to the staff.

"What is going on? Where is Erin Whitmeyer?" she demanded. "Why can't we see her?" I could not make out the muffled response. She continued, her loud voice carrying easily through the walls. "Why aren't we being told anything about her condition? I want to know what is going on now!"

This is exactly why I wanted her to come with me.

My body was numb, and my mind swirled as my world began to process an unthinkable new possibility.

They would be giving us an update if she were okay. They are preparing to break the news to us.

As the hospital chaplain entered, the waiting room suddenly grew smaller. Dea's voice pounded in my head along with every new piece of information that was altering my world, a world that was about to stand still. The drumbeats grew louder. Finally, she returned and murmured to me, "We can go in." I grabbed her hand as she showed me the way.

We walked a short distance down the hall and stopped at a closed door. I looked at Dea's somber face and felt the air change. I knew in an instant I wasn't going to like what awaited me on the other side of that door. A nurse pushed the door open for us, looking equally somber, and I turned to enter the glare of the well-lit room. I was instantly thrust into a scene I wanted to run from.

My Erin was lying perfectly still on the gurney that had carried her out of our house. Her eyes were closed, her arms no longer locked but lying straight at her sides. At first glance she appeared to be sleeping, but she was too still and so very pale.

No.

The soft-pink flush of her cheeks was long gone. Her normally soft-pink lips were colorless. I recalled a similar horrific moment a year earlier when my dad had suddenly passed away. My heart began to beat faster now, so quickly; I thought it would burst from my chest.

"We will give you some time with Erin," the doctor said. I hadn't even realized there was a doctor in the room with us.

"Dea, do something! Can't you do something?" I was frantic. Each person dressed in white filed out of the room, and I asked Dea, "Where are they going? Where are they taking her next? Don't they need to do some tests?" Dea, being the friend that Erin loved, turned to look at me with sorrow and gently put her hand on my arm.

"They're not taking her anywhere, John. Erin is gone."

The words hung in the air as I sank to my knees at Erin's bedside. During my descent, my forehead brushed against the very thigh I had once innocently touched to make sure she was real.

Instinctively I held on to her and began to absorb this crushing blow. In the blink of an eye, a split second in time, I was here, and she was gone. My clock was still ticking, but my life had stopped with Erin's breathing. In that moment, I became just half of a man as I felt my other half ripped from this shell I called me.

I was always prepared and willing to love her but never prepared to say goodbye. *Although we promised "till death do us part," we never imagined the parting.*

How could I allow myself to love something so much? Pulsing violence ripped through me as I attempted to process the unfathomable.

No.

My love for Erin was magnified as I replayed my epic failure. *I didn't save her.*

This person I adored, the very source of everything good in my life was now gone because I failed to do what was needed to save her. *If I had done something differently, she might still be here with us.*

My thoughts turned to those who loved her. *I failed them too.*

Because of my inability to save her, all those people were now going to suffer as well. Pushed from darkness into murky waters, staying afloat seemed impossible. I immediately felt as if I was drifting among all those who loved Erin, lifeless, living with pain greater than any I had ever faced in my life.

Like a desperate, frightened child, I held her cold hand and draped my lifeless arm across her body. Resting my head on her, I wept. I would not and could not accept this. It just couldn't be real. I was broken to pieces. Loving her was always easy because she gave me so many reasons to cherish her. Just as I would my own children, I would have given my life to have her back.

An emotional storm engulfed every crevice of my fractured mind as I struggled to process what had happened. Every second that continued to pass rang loudly in my ears. Clutching her hand, I longed for it to become warm again. I longed for Erin to warm my now-frozen heart as she had done for so many years.

To have and to hold her—isn't that what I promised?

Once again, I felt myself float up out of my body. Perhaps this was my mind's way of helping me to escape that which I could not bear. I wondered if I was even alive myself. Surely Erin was in heaven, and I felt like I'd been transported straight to hell, so empty, so hollow. The me that existed just moments ago was now gone. I didn't know this new me, and I didn't want to. With Erin's death, my ability to distinguish what was real had become impaired.

What time was it?

Time no longer mattered. At some point through the dark fog of my mind, I became dimly aware of other voices in the room. They were the voices of Erin's parents, brother, and sister. I had no idea how long they had been there.

"This can't be happening. This can't be happening," I repeated over and over to myself. I felt the warmth of the chaplain's hand on my shoulder. I was unaware he had been standing behind me the whole time.

I thought of Erin and her magical ways, how easily she put people at ease and made them feel special. I thought of her warm light and how it made everything better. I hoped beyond all logic that she would be able to pull it off once more.

Couldn't she somehow make this better?

I kept my head down because I didn't have the strength to lift it. I felt deserted. My mind sifted through the friends in her inner circle. As I imagined each of their faces painted with pain, I realized that for this fleeting moment, each of her friends were sleeping at home, oblivious to this evening's events, and Erin was still alive in their worlds. That would change very soon when they, too, received the devastating blow that Erin was gone.

Erin was gone.

Seconds turned to minutes which then turned to hours. I didn't want the time with her to end. These final moments would be cherished forever because it would be the last time I would touch this precious girl, Erin, who now lay before me in empty silence.

Where did she go? The answer was beyond me.

It was time to say goodbye. I wasn't ready, and I certainly couldn't do it alone. It was push and pull to get me to leave that room as the nursing staff delicately but firmly showed us the door. I spilled out of the room into a long, gloomy hallway.

For an all too brief moment, I could see Erin skipping and laughing her way down a similar hallway, blonde curls bouncing as she popped in and out of the rooms in our college dorm. That was twenty-four years earlier when I first laid eyes on my beautiful girl. While the hallway at college that led me to her felt inviting, this hallway, in stark contrast, was bleak and overwhelmingly endless, leading me away from my love.

How can I take these steps without Erin by my side? How do I just walk away from her?

Stumbling forward, I left the best part of myself behind in that room. With every step, the distance between us and the fear within me grew. I'd never felt more alone or abandoned. My shattered mind was stuck on instant replay, and each take cut deeply into my flesh.

CHAPTER 2

DESPERATION AND DESPAIR

I HAD BEEN CRYING for hours. Devastated beyond human comprehension, I slowly began to realize I had lost sight of the three people most important to me—our children. New waves of shame washed over me and merged with my shock and horror. I walked down the hallway of the hospital away from Erin and toward what remained of our life together—the most precious, innocent, vulnerable parts of our life together—our children.

I finally realized they had been left alone for hours with Pat with no updates and no idea what had happened. The sickening realization began to creep in that I now had to tell my three young children their mother had died, and they would never see her again.

Oh my god.

Erin's brother John and I sped home in the quiet night. John had been kind enough to offer me a ride, and I was wise enough to accept it. The ride was silent; each of us were immersed in the emotional noise of our internal storms.

How am I going to find the strength to look into our children's eyes and completely destroy them? How can I possibly tell them their mother died tonight?

John pulled into the driveway as the first hints of dawn streaked across the sky. We looked at each other with silent understanding. No words were needed. He reached out and briefly rested his hand on my shoulder in an offering of comfort and strength. I nodded my appreciation and, opening the car door, stepped out to face the unthinkable.

I walked slowly down the driveway, a broken man pushing my way through interchanging feelings of grief, dread, shame, anger, and horror. When I reached the back door, I rested my hand on the doorknob for a long moment and took a deep, fortifying breath. Exhaling, I turned the knob, pushed open the door, and stepped into another of the most difficult moments I had ever been faced with.

Brittany and Johnny were sitting in the family room with Pat. They were in the very spot where I last saw their mother alive.

She spoke her last words to me from that very spot on the couch.

Pat must have seen it all in my face because without a word, he discreetly slipped out of the room, offering me time alone with my children.

Kylie was not home yet. I sat down on the couch with Brittany, and Johnny stood sleepily before me in his favorite blue pj's. I protectively put my arm around him, wanting to shield him from the news I was about to share. They both stared expectantly at me, traces of fear in their eyes.

"Where is Mommy?" Brittany searched my face for a sign of hope. "Is she okay? When is she coming home?"

"Mommy isn't coming home." The words tumbled out. I couldn't take them back, and I couldn't leave them just hanging there with no further explanation. I had to continue. Appallingly, I heard myself say, "Mommy died tonight."

After a stunned second, my children burst into tears as their worst fears were realized. I broke down under the intensity of their pain. Their mother was gone forever. I held them, helpless, as they cried in my arms, and I cried right along with them. Our world as we once knew it had changed forever.

Word traveled quickly, and within an hour, our house and yard were filled with a hundred people. Neighbors, Erin's friends, and family—all gathered around us as they heard the devastating news.

The sunshine was deceivingly bright on such a dark day. I was anxiously awaiting the arrival of Kylie who was being brought home by a family friend. The devastation of the last few hours continued as I prepared myself to tell another one of my children her mother had died. Kylie was deeply connected with her mother, and I was especially worried about how she would take the news. I froze for a moment as I heard the back door open.

"What's going on? Is my Dad okay?" Kylie blurted out as she entered the house. Clearly confused by the sight of so many people gathered in her home, she scanned the crowd in search of her mother. Erin's sister Shannon went over to her and gently guided Kylie over to us in the family room.

"Dad, what's going on? I thought something happened to you! Why are all these people here?" Kylie asked. Her big, blue eyes were especially wide as she recognized the assortment of people who had gathered.

My eyes welled with tears as I looked helplessly at her beautifully innocent face. I simply could not find the parental strength in that moment to tell my daughter that she would never see her mother again. Shannon watched this exchange, and recognizing my inability, she instinctively stepped in for me and took on the unimaginable task.

"Come sit here with us, Kylie. We want to talk to you." Kylie's brows furrowed a bit, just like her mother's did when she was confused, and my breath caught in my throat.

She walked warily over to the couch and sat down. Shannon sat on the coffee table facing her and took both of Kylie's hands into hers. Kylie looked uncomfortable.

"Kylie, something happened to Mom last night. We're not sure what exactly happened. It might have been an asthma attack, but we don't know for sure yet."

"Oh no!" Kylie's eyes widened again. "Is she okay now? Where is she? Is she in the hospital?" Her eyes scanned the crowd of people milling around the house. "Or is she home, and all these people are visiting her?" Her voice trailed off as she tried to piece it together. Shannon's matching blue eyes brimmed with tears as she looked at her niece.

"Kylie, she died. She's gone."

Kylie blinked, stunned by the words as they sank in. The color drained from her face. She sat in frozen silence as we all put our arms around her. We were finally all together, but there were four of us now instead of five. Our collective tears flowed.

The house continued to fill with friends, coworkers, neighbors, and family. I made my way through the crowd to a chair in the living room and collapsed into it, dazed. People wandered from room to room trying to keep themselves busy. Everyone wanted to help in some way. I was oblivious to what was happening around me.

My mind automatically searched for Erin around every corner. I expected to see her walking down the stairs into the living room or to look over and see her standing with a group of friends laughing and catching up.

She should be here to see this. She would be amazed. So many people loved her.

I tried to keep visual tabs on the kids. Whenever I saw them, they were surrounded by a swarm of friends. I wanted to go to them and pull them close to me, but I knew in this moment, they needed their friends. They were so much like their mother in that way. I kept an eye on them from afar in the event they faltered and needed me.

At one point, I watched in confusion as a friend approached Johnny with a gift. Johnny looked equally confused.

"We brought this for you because we were going to give it to you today at your birthday party," the boy's mother quietly explained. Johnny bravely tried to smile as he graciously accepted the gift.

"Thank you," he said quietly.

Oh my god. Erin had planned Johnny's eighth birthday party for today. The blows just kept coming one after the other.

Our friends and family had no idea what to say to me.

Who could blame them? I don't know what to say to them either.

My lively girl, who had just been happily swinging her tennis racket in this very room a few hours ago, had simply vanished.

Gone forever.

My grief began closing in on me. I closed my eyes, and I saw her standing right there in front of me. I could hear her talking to me and laughing with me, but when I opened my eyes, she faded away, and I was once again shattered into tiny pieces. My mind couldn't stop replaying my futile efforts to revive her and the vision of her lifeless body jumping from the floor. I sat dazed.

I'm responsible for this. All of this is my fault.

The unbearable weight of my guilt pressed me even further into the depths of despair, threatening to crush me. I was still among the living, but without Erin, I no longer felt alive.

Time slowly dripped through me, and after several hours, I finally whispered to a friend that it was time for everyone to go. I couldn't process anymore. I couldn't talk anymore. I needed to be alone.

My sisters had arrived sometime during the morning to offer support and help me care for the kids. The hours dragged on, and as the sun was finally setting on this horrible day, I badly needed to rest. I reassured my children that I was nearby, just in the next room, and left them in the loving care of my sisters as I escaped to the welcome solitude of my room.

It then occured to me that this was the very scene of utter devastation just hours before. Whatever thoughts, feelings, or images that may have attempted to surface about the events taking place in the bedroom the previous night were immediately and effectively pushed back down into the deepest recesses of my mind.

Not now. I can't deal with that now.

As I had always done, I tiptoed over to my side of the bed, carefully pulled back the covers, and climbed in as quietly as possible, fearful of waking Erin. I tried to recover my breathing as quietly as I could and was careful to keep my icy cold feet on my side, gently rubbing them together for warmth. A train horn sounded in the distance, and reflective lights from a passing car danced across the walls of our bedroom.

There she was at the end of a long hallway, darting from one room to another. The hallway turned darker as I began walking toward her. Afraid she would leave before I could reach her, I began to run. As I neared the first doorway, I turned and looked into the glare of a well-lit room. Erin was lying on the bed, hand outstretched to me.

Her face was pale, no trace of the usual pink flush in her cheeks. Her colorless mouth was struggling to form words, but nothing came out.

Sickened, I turned and ran away. I came upon the next doorway and forced myself to look into the glare. She was lying there, just like before, hand outstretched, colorless mouth speaking soundless words. I ran. Doorway after doorway offered the same horrifying apparition. My weak legs propelled me on, and I squeezed my eyes shut, running with everything I had.

No.

My eyes snapped open, and for a split second, it felt like any other morning. The first wave of reality washed over me, and it hit hard. Like a painful punch to the gut, the air was knocked from my lungs as horrific flashes of memory from the past twenty-four hours quickly resurfaced.

No.

Without turning my head to look, I stretched my arm across the bed, willing my hand to come in contact with Erin's warm arm. It was instead greeted by the cool, smooth, empty sheets of Erin's side of the bed. Another wave of reality and grief washed over me, knocking me under. An agonized moan escaped my throat as I realized the previous day's nightmare continued.

The morning sun highlighted Erin's belongings, and I just wanted to hold her again. I grabbed her pillow and squeezed it to my chest, burying my face in it. It smelled like her. A single excruciating sob escaped me, and with it was released an uncontrollable torrent of weeping.

No.

I cried out heavy tears, until her pillow was soaked with my grief. When I could finally bring myself to fully open my eyes to this day, the first thing they focused on was her green sweater from the night before, folded neatly on the chair where she had left it.

Her idle tennis racket leaned against the wall, now no longer a threat to its surroundings. I turned to look at our wedding picture proudly displayed over our bed, the day we became one.

We never imagined the parting.

The muffled sounds of children's voices and clanking dishes vibrated up through the floor, telling me that the kids were awake, and my sisters were preparing them breakfast.

Our children.

I sat up. That was the motivation I needed to start this day.

Our children need me. I'm their only remaining parent.

I wanted time to move quickly now, but it didn't. Pain seems more crippling when time moves slowly. *Oh my god, I have to buy Erin a headstone.* A horrifying thought, as I contemplated crawling under my own. I held on for dear life through this turbulence. I was stripped of everything that shielded me, forced to accept the naked truth. Why couldn't it have been me? Fear surrounded me. My heart was filled with sorrow for her severed life.

She was so young, so healthy, so full of life. How could this have happened? We were awaiting the autopsy results, hoping they would help to make sense of what had happened to our Erin.

I dragged myself out of bed, and with the heaviest limbs and heart, I started the first full day of my new life. My sisters gathered around, offering me their thoughtful considerations. Kathy made her traditional big family breakfast of eggs, bacon, bagels, and coffee. I took some comfort knowing family was with us, yet sudden aftershocks of grief targeted each of us without warning and threatened to shatter our already fragile worlds. I watched as the children moved through the morning and was comforted seeing them holding up better than expected.

I knew I had to pull myself together and go to the funeral home to decide on arrangements for Erin's wake. How do people do these things? How can they possibly function? At some point the phone rang. It was the Coroner himself, calling with news we were all anxiously awaiting.

"John, I want to give you a status update. I have thoroughly examined the heart and all other major organs, and so far, I have found nothing conclusive as to cause of death. I expect to complete the physical examination today. The toxicology results will take several more weeks. I will follow up with you as soon as I am finished here today."

Nothing conclusive.

It was time to go to the funeral home. My shoes felt glued to the floor, and moving forward through these preparations seemed impossible.

Erin's family and I were greeted at the front door by Jim, the funeral director. He was a kind and courteous man, and I could sense he was experienced in dealing with situations like ours. He escorted us to a beautiful conference room. It seemed ludicrous sitting in a plush, comfortable room to have the most uncomfortable conversation of my life. Jim expertly offered his condolences and his professionalism, and I appreciated both. He handled us with great care and sensitivity.

Jim confirmed that Erin was in Farmington for an autopsy. I still couldn't wrap my head around the fact that my wife was no longer here. Farmington felt worlds away. I hadn't known exactly where she was, an idea that had been foreign to me for over two decades. We always checked in with each other; we always knew where the other was. She was slipping even further away, and I was struggling to hold on.

I pulled myself back to the grim task at hand and became fixated on making sure every detail of Erin's wake and funeral was carefully considered.

Years before, we had made similar decisions about flowers, color schemes, and readings as we planned our wedding to be the most perfect day of our lives. Now I was planning my bride's funeral.

All the decisions she could no longer make for herself were now left to me. How could I possibly decide on a coffin? My wife would really be lying in that? I was horrified at the thought yet had to make this a beautiful send-off, a funeral fit for someone as special as Erin.

Hundreds of people loved her, and I had no doubt that many would be coming to honor her. Once the details for the funeral had been decided upon, we headed home, drained.

My thoughts shifted from my own loss and suffering to the well-being of my children. How would I find the strength to ease their pain when my own was all-encompassing? Clearly the worst imaginable pain was being felt in their young hearts. I wanted to take it all away. As I tried to convince myself that I could find the strength to comfort them and that I could guide them through this grief, I crumbled, cradling my head in my own hands and sobbing for what would no longer be.

When I entered the house, I looked for my children. I found them sitting comfortably together in the family room with my sister Sue watching a movie. It almost looked like a normal scene on any other day. Because it was far from any other day, I quickly scanned their faces for telltale signs of crying, anger, or fear. They looked tired but surprisingly calm. No tears but the mood was subdued.

Sue looked knowingly at me and softly asked how it went. I nodded and mumbled something incoherent. She frowned a bit as she scanned my face.

"We're okay, just watching a good movie. Why don't you go lie down for a bit and get some rest?" I looked again at my children and satisfied that they were in the care of their loving Aunt Sue. I went up to my bedroom to lie down.

I collapsed onto the bed, pulled a pillow over my head and attempted to shut out the blaring thoughts and gut-wrenching images of events that took place in this very same spot where I was now supposed to rest. I sobbed.

I opened my eyes on day two, the day we were to celebrate Erin. I lie in bed staring up at the ceiling, thinking again about how cruel it was that her life had ended so prematurely. I thought of all the important moments she would never get to share with her children—proms, graduations, weddings, grandchildren. More sobbing.

Erin and I had laid the groundwork for this life and were looking forward to enjoying these priceless milestones together. She had been robbed of seeing her children grow up. They had been robbed of having their mother with them through the most exciting and challenging years of their young lives. They would not have her unconditional love and support to help guide them through life's challenges. They only had me.

As the morning progressed, friends and family members began to gather at our home once again. As I emerged from my protective cocoon upstairs, I heard the hushed tones as they all reverently planned for the details of Erin's celebration. I wandered aimlessly through the rooms, doing my best to greet everyone and express my appreciation for their presence and their efforts and have it sound sincere. Inside I was hollow.

I glanced over and saw Erin's childhood friends, the kids, and my sisters pouring over photos. I noticed that some favorite family photos had been taken down from the walls throughout the house where Erin had hung them. I panicked a bit as I felt her disappearing all over again. I reminded myself that our friends and family were working hard to ensure a beautiful ceremony that honored every poignant phase of her life. It was important for them to express their love for Erin in this way as they, too, came to terms with their own grief.

Through the fog of my own fragmented thoughts, I suddenly felt compelled to write something for her. I slipped back up to the quiet solitude of my room, pen and paper in hand. For some time, I stared at the clean paper, gathering my thoughts and blending them with my emotions in what I hoped would be a cohesive message to my love. Forever for us had now come and gone. I'd keep it simple, speaking from the heart. Perhaps my feelings would flow with my tears.

Erin's friends had taken on the task of choosing her last outfit, and it was now time for me to choose an outfit for myself. How could I think about what to wear when I felt like an empty shell laying alone in the sand? I chose a gray suit to match my mood and a blood-red tie, perhaps in an unconscious nod to my bleeding heart. I felt so cold. Would my heart be warm enough to allow me to sincerely greet the mourners who would be coming to offer their condolences and see her off?

I can't do this.

The phone rang. It was Lindsey, Erin's good friend and hairstylist. She was at the funeral home helping to prepare Erin for the viewing. Her words made my blood run cold.

"John, I just want to warn you that Erin doesn't look like herself." There was a slight awkward pause. "In fact, she looks strikingly different." Evidently the invasive autopsy had altered Erin's appearance, another unforeseen blow. I never longed for a day to be over more than this one.

Later as I pulled my car into the funeral home parking lot, I realized that I'd driven by this entrance countless times, never imagining I would be pulling in today for this reason. I quickly glanced at Brittany, Kylie, and Johnny. They were sitting quietly, faces somber. Their eyes hinted at their fear and weariness. Our children had been surprisingly strong over the past couple of days, much more composed than I ever could have imagined, more composed than me. They were too young to be going through this level of trauma and grief.

We entered the long foyer of the funeral home with Erin's parents, brother, sister, my mother, and my sisters. As we walked into the ornate silence, I clutched my children closely, and the funeral director approached.

Jim greeted us with a warm smile. I knew he had experienced this kind of greeting countless times and had most likely seen the dazed expressions and trembling hands many times over, yet he made us feel like we were the only family who had experienced such a devastating loss. I was grateful for him in that moment. I noticed we instinctively spoke in whispers as if we might wake Erin up.

If only it were that easy.

Jim invited my children and me to sit on one of the lavishly upholstered benches that adorned the center of the room. We waited there for additional family to arrive. There was no sign of Erin, and it was an odd realization that she was lying alone in the next room, and we were all out here. My children and I sat in numb silence. I swallowed hard, imagining the awful scene they were about to face. I steadied myself, realizing they were going to need to see my strength in order to feel safe and get through the next couple of hours.

Within a few seconds, my mother appeared and sat on the bench across from us. I did not feel the comfort one might normally feel when their mother attempts to console them. To say our relationship was strained would be an understatement. I felt my defenses kicking in and my protective walls shot up. My mother made a feeble attempt to comfort me, a gesture that was strangely foreign, and I felt enraged.

Not now, Barbara.

To me she appeared needy and insincere, and I was in no frame of mind to accommodate any of this. I resented her for drawing my attention and energy to her and away from those who truly needed and deserved it—Erin and our children. I could only glare at her and bite my lip hard with anger.

"Go on in, Mom," I said abruptly to her, redirecting all my attention back to my children.

We were offered a private viewing to spend time with Erin before the doors opened to the rest of our friends and family. The cars had already started to arrive, carrying those who came to say their last farewells to their beloved friend who had gone too soon.

We walked into the main parlor and saw Erin's lifeless body lying there alone. The photos from our home, carefully selected by her friends and our family, were arranged on display boards around the room, offering a brief visual history of Erin's life from infancy through to our most recent days together. Flowers of every color, shape, and size surrounded her casket. Their vibrance was in direct contrast with Erin's current state and how I felt inside.

I trembled as we approached the casket. I hadn't seen her since that horrific morning at the hospital, and my children hadn't seen her since they said good night two nights before. The stark change in her appearance must have been shocking for them, to say the least. I was stunned by the sight of her, and Lindsey's words echoed in my mind. "She doesn't look like herself."

I remembered what the coroner had said the night before when he finally called me back with the final autopsy results. His voice had been strained, and he sounded exhausted.

"John, in my twenty-year career, this is the first time I was not able to pinpoint a cause of death. Keep in mind, we are still awaiting the results of toxicology, but I could find nothing physically wrong with Erin. There is no determinable cause of death at this point. I'm sorry I can't give you a more conclusive explanation."

I now stared down at Erin's distorted face and could clearly tell that the coroner had worked very diligently to find the elusive reason for her death. The mortician and Lindsey had tried to conceal evidence of the invasive investigation, yet the result was that she was almost totally unrecognizable. I shuddered and fought back thoughts of what my beautiful girl must have had been put through. The idea was appalling. We all huddled closer, and I whispered a silent prayer over her lifeless body, hoping that she was in a better place and that she had no idea what her body had been through.

I dug deep and found the strength to pull myself together for our children, the three who represented the love between me and my bride. Tears welled in their eyes as they, too, fought to be strong. We arranged ourselves in an orderly receiving line, although on the inside, disorder threatened to destroy us.

I made sure the children sat with my sisters. I did not want them having to put on brave faces and greet hundreds of people in their time of grief. Erin's parents would be the first to greet the mourners. I situated myself between her mother and her brother.

Soon the viewing was under way. The mourners filed in, and within minutes, the line of people spilled out into the parking lot and wrapped around the building. I was oblivious to this at the time as my sole focus was to sincerely greet each person one at a time and thank them each for coming. I shook hands and offered hugs to every single person, choking back tears.

Calling hours were originally set for four hours, but Erin's love of people and love of life kept us there an additional two. I would stand there for as long as it took to thank every single person for coming to pay their respects. These people loved Erin and felt the numbing blow of her loss as we did. Out loud I spoke the words, "Thanks for coming," but my soul whispered, "I'm sorry I failed you."

After six exhausting hours, my sisters took the children home, and it occurred to me that this would be the last time I would see Erin. Ever.

Cautiously I approached my wife for the last time. She lay there looking peaceful while I felt the violence of my world with her being ripped away. My joints ached with physical pain from this trying day. That pain was nothing compared to the aching in my heart for my beautiful girl, my best friend, my partner.

I stared at her and let this last moment with her soak in. How many times had I stared at this lovely face as we engaged in conversations about life? How many expressions had I seen play across it over the years? Love, tenderness, humor, anger, frustration, and admiration—her face had expressed it all. I had seen myself reflected there for over twenty years as Erin responded to me and helped to shape the man I was.

I thought of those quiet, unaware moments when her face took on a softness and a glow that was indescribably beautiful. I recalled the look of contentment and nurturing warmth it exuded when she looked at her children. This beautifully expressive face that had once been the main window to Erin's soul was now oddly still and lifeless. It reflected nothing.

I stared, half expecting her to move or take a breath. She didn't. I didn't know how I could go on without her, my classy girl with her hair done just so, dressed beautifully in a ruffled, pink blouse, bright-blue Lucky jeans, and of course, her favorite Jimmy Choos.

Her friends chose her last outfit well. She would have loved it.

Pictures and notes from our children surrounded her, such beauty all encased in sadness as she lay so morbidly still. I was overcome with grief. The words I had written to her that morning had been printed and placed in the casket with her.

"My friend, my wife, my love. In all my travels to come, I will never sense another force as strong and beautiful as you. Please accept this piece of me to hold tightly until we can be together again. I will hold you in my heart forever. Our love so pure, I will cherish it for eternity."

This girl, Erin, the one I had grown to love deeper than my own life, was gone. Tomorrow I would bury Erin in this beautiful casket, putting her into the ground forever. I bowed my head as if in prayer, but a prayer wasn't spoken because my prayers apparently went unanswered.

"I'm sorry that I didn't act more quickly and that I let you slip away. It's my fault you are gone. I was supposed to take care of you, and I failed. I don't know if I can ever forgive myself." I reached for her cold hand, and I held it for a moment, unsure of how to say goodbye. I would never again see my true love.

God, can even You imagine my pain?

The next morning, I opened my eyes, and a heavy wave of dread washed over me. The funeral day had arrived. The previous night's viewing had left us all weary emotionally, mentally, and physically. Today promised to be no less daunting.

Erin was the only reason I was able to get through these last few days. She was always able to see the strength in me, even when I couldn't feel it myself, and I knew she would expect me to push through this and be a source of strength and stability for our children. Lifting myself from my lonely bed, so began the day my wife was to be buried in the ground. I robotically reached for pants, a shirt, and shoes. I chose an appropriately dark tie to complete the outfit.

The limousine pulled into the driveway like an ominous shadow. My stomach sank as we reluctantly climbed in, preparing to be transported to the final goodbye. I wanted to be sick. I glanced around at my family; their pained expressions mirrored my own raw feelings.

As we backed out of the driveway, I noticed a beautiful pink ribbon on our mailbox.

"Dad! Look!" Kylie exclaimed, pointing. This was yet another thoughtful gesture from someone who loved the girl that I loved too. As we headed down the street, we noticed the same ceremonial pink ribbon on every single mailbox in our neighborhood.

"Look at all of them! Who did that?" Brittany's eyes were wide as she craned her head to see.

"That is so nice. Your mom is loved," I replied softly. This show of solidarity overwhelmed us. We felt the warmth of the loving message it conveyed, and for a moment, the darkness was dispelled. I fought back tears of gratitude.

Erin, you earned every one of these. This is a testament to who you are.

We pulled up to the church as distraught mourners filed in. Our line of limousines arrived last with Erin, as she did in life, leading our pack. We climbed out of the back of our limousine, and my children and I held hands in support of one another as we slowly entered the somber, crowded church.

People were crammed in the pews and huddled closely together around the nave of the church. We slowly proceeded down the central aisle, following Erin's beautiful casket, embellished with colorful flowers. Our family filled the first few pews on the right side, our close friends on the left, and my children and I took our seats in the front row. I found myself thrust into a role and a position I neither chose nor wanted. Focusing only on what was in front of me, the shame I felt wouldn't allow me to look around.

I listened to the priest singing Erin's praises. He told us that God had a plan for her, and we must rejoice in this plan. I heard his words, and they sounded like empty noise. Erin and I had a plan too; our plans were for Erin to be here with us. Our children desperately needed her. I needed her.

My mind struggled to stay focused on the service as I continued to process my own internal horrors. I was not impressed with the words I was hearing. They did not comfort me. In fact, I felt scorned. How could anyone be rejoicing when I no longer had my wife and my children were now motherless? Anger, resentment, and shame overtook my mind and heart in God's house, and I was too weak to push them away.

Four of Erin's very best high-school friends took to the pulpit, and each took a moment to reminisce about their memories with Erin. It had been some time since they had seen each other, yet their words painted a collective picture of Erin's spunkiness, her humor, and her strength of character. The tributes were beautiful and sincere, and they evoked laughter as well as tears. Their personal stories allowed us to revisit happier days and to once again bask in Erin's light. I made eye contact with each friend to let them know how grateful we were for their words. When the service had ended, we all filed out in solemn silence, following closely behind Erin, and headed toward the awaiting limousines.

The mourners followed somberly, some taking to their cars, and some choosing to walk over to the cemetery despite the brisk early March weather. Erin's final resting place was just a short distance away. Erin's hearse had gone ahead so the funeral-home staff could get her casket situated before everyone else arrived.

As our car pulled up, we saw a huge crowd had gathered around Erin. There were a few chairs set up for our immediate family. My children and I trudged slowly across the brown lawn, clinging to each other for support.

As the priest made his final comments, muffled sobs were carried forth on the bitter winter breeze, and I drew my sorrow inward once again. Weak and feeble, I held my children close. I felt the weight of the suffering that was now surrounding us. I felt pain with every sincere handshake; every condolence offered in kindness tore me up inside. And each time the priest said that Erin was a gift to God, I felt more alone.

She had been my gift.

I needed Erin back. She was strong for me when I was not. She gave me direction when I was lost. She helped me to stand when I had fallen. I looked at our children and noted their little faces tinged with sorrow. I knew it would break Erin's heart to see her babies suffering in this way. The direction of their happy, innocent lives had been forever altered, and I had never known such heartache. I had never been as ready for a door to close on a day as I was in that moment. At the same time, ironically, my life had suddenly taken on new meaning. As much as I could not fathom doing so without Erin, I needed to live. My children needed me.

Chapter 3

It Should Have Been Me

For some time now, given the current state of my health, it was assumed I would pass on first. At least it was assumed until a few weeks prior when Erin was told something different by the psychic. It was supposed to be me. I had already been presented with the difficult prospect of facing my own death.

As a result of my weakening physical condition, I had started to rely heavily on Erin just to get through the basics of each day, and this was beginning to take a toll on us.

We had three young children, and I had, until recently, been an extremely self-driven, hyperactive workaholic with multiple projects under way at any given moment. Now I found myself barely able to get to work, let alone continue to maintain the multiple properties we owned, collect rents, and find tenants like I was used to doing.

After several years of overall success, Erin had acquired a taste for the good life. The housing bubble that would devastate our country's economy now loomed over us and threatened the way of life we had become accustomed to. The truth was, financially we were sinking fast, and Erin blamed me. Our conversations grew more hostile as we began to feel the squeeze financially from the three homes we owned. I began to question my ability to provide for my own family. When the pressure mounted, Erin would remind me through clenched teeth, "This was *your* dream!"

Some days I felt as though Erin wanted to shake me, hoping that would make me feel better so we could get our life back. Our bond was breaking down. I felt useless physically, and it began to affect the way I felt about myself mentally, a dangerous position to be in.

"Can we make it?" Erin would ask.

"I can't make it without you," I replied each time. I loved this girl, and my feelings hadn't changed just because I was sick.

Now after Erin's sudden passing, I could see very clearly that dying was actually easy. It was living that was difficult. I now faced my own battle with death alone, without the woman I could never lose.

I wandered aimlessly through each passing day like an abandoned child who had lost his way. Mentally I knew all too well that Erin was gone, but everywhere I turned, there she was. She was there in Kylie's blonde hair and smile. Johnny looked at me with her beautiful blue eyes. Brittany's thoughtfulness and nurturing ways were quintessentially Erin. Everyday objects took on new reverence.

Erin touched that last. She placed that there. Something as simple as her handwritten note on the fridge was enough to break me.

My mind was consumed with replays of the darkest scenes of Erin's death and my own self-perceived failures leading up to it. I dwelled there in those horrifying moments, unable to move forward. The healthy, vibrant person I lived through was gone. Why was I still here? My personal flaws quickly rose to the surface of my thoughts, and although I wanted nothing more than to hide from them, I found myself unable to let them go or move past them. I didn't deserve to be here. It should have been me. I was already sick.

Two years earlier on a beautiful spring morning, Brittany and I had decided to have a catch. It was some early conditioning to prepare for her upcoming softball season. I was moving much slower and was a year older, but it was normal to tighten up during the winter months.

"Step into it, Britt," I instructed as we threw to each other back and forth. Brittany threw the ball hard, and I was surprised by a throw that landed in front of me as it bounced off the side of my knee. I collapsed to the ground, wincing in pain as it shot right through me. I took a minute to recover, then we went inside. Softball conditioning was finished for the day. I hobbled around that afternoon, unaware that the pain I was feeling was actually the beginning of something much worse.

I woke up the next morning and thought I'd slept in the wrong position because my neck was painfully stiff, and moving my head from side to side was a struggle. Not thinking much about it, I went on with my day. The neck pain, though, never subsided and was reminiscent of a similar occurrence from when I was young.

My body had declared war for the first time right before the start of my freshman year of high school when I was blindsided by a mysterious and debilitating condition.

What appeared to be simply growing pains became increasingly painful and quickly spread throughout my body. It was most pronounced in my hips and knees, and eventually all my joints ached. The excruciating pain hindered my sleep. There wasn't a comfortable spot that I could find on my mattress. I would get out of bed in the morning hardly able to walk, struggled to brush my teeth, and could barely get a comb through my hair. Most nights I'd just lie in the dark, sobbing quietly, fearful of what might be happening to me. I knew it was not normal.

The excruciating pain throughout my body was so severe that I missed the first day of high school. It was difficult to walk, and I was scared. My condition worsened with each passing day, and my parents took me to the doctor. After a thorough exam and comprehensive blood work, the doctors still looked perplexed. *Transient arthritis* was the best they could come up with. All tests were inconclusive.

Over the next three months, I began each day the same way. My legs were weak; my hips were stiff and sore, and my fingers were painfully curled up, only straightening out over a period of hours. Was this how I would live the remainder of my life? I was angry inside, and depression began to set in.

As I limped around school, I selfishly looked at others and wondered, "Why me and not you?" My physical limitations were not immediately obvious to others, but my resentment intensified.

I lacked basic coping skills that might have helped me process this experience in a healthy way. Instead, I bottled it all up and didn't tell anyone I was suffering. I didn't want the attention or pity of my classmates and teachers. I just wanted to be like everyone else. The pain and isolation left me feeling hopeless.

Then as suddenly as it had appeared, the mysterious pain was gone. I resumed my normal life, and that three months of agony became a distant blip on the radar.

Although eerily similar, the pain I was feeling now as an adult was much more intense than it had been when I was fourteen. I began to worry. Slowing down was a new feeling for me, a strange feeling. Resuming a normal life seemed daunting. My mind and my body worked in opposite directions.

The constant drone of pain affected everything I did. I became irritable and had little patience. It was difficult to focus, and my thoughts became muddied. The pressure of my obligations mounted as I felt less and less able to manage them. I was scared, but I didn't want anyone to know. I needed to be strong for Erin and my children because they were growing concerned too.

I was deteriorating fast. I went from doctor to doctor in a frantic effort to find someone who could tell me what was wrong. Each doctor I saw presented the same diagnosis; nothing was wrong. Each blood test revealed nothing. I had been convinced it was Lyme disease; the tests came up negative each time.

My strength diminished rapidly, and I began having difficulty breathing. A simple walk of a few short feet resulted in my having to sit and catch my breath. My legs felt like they were weighed down by cement blocks. I was weakest in my thighs. The day I had to ask my five-year-old son, Johnny, to help me sit up was a new low for me.

Erin was adept at confronting problems head-on, and I had learned this skill from her. Now because of my declining health, we found ourselves faced with problems that seemed to have no solution. Something we were not accustomed to.

I worried about her. She looked tired. I could see she was pushing herself harder each day to take care of the children, me, the house, and all the other obligations that swirled around us. She was also working full time. Erin was someone who needed to cut loose and have some fun occasionally; those days seemed a distant memory.

Our friends and our family had no idea about the severity of our situation, and I'm not sure why, but we instinctively hid our problems from everyone around us.

Finally, about three months into this painful journey, we were offered a glimmer of hope. I was referred to a highly respected infectious disease specialist, who happened to be local. Surely he would be able to give us the answers we were so desperately seeking.

The examination proved at first to be no different than the others I had already experienced. The doctor agreed that my symptoms looked very much like Lyme disease, just as I had suspected initially. Unlike my previous doctors, he was authorized to administer the Western blot test, reportedly a much more accurate test for Lyme disease. I was hopeful. The blood-test results would take several days. He started me on a course of antibiotics right away, the standard protocol for Lyme disease. I was encouraged.

Around this time, Erin and the kids had an opportunity to go to the Jersey shore with Erin's good friend, Dea. Erin was hesitant to leave me, but given the hope of finally getting some answers for the first time in months, I felt optimistic about the future. I insisted that she take the children, go have some fun, and escape from the daily stresses of watching me deteriorate. They desperately needed some time away, and I knew Erin needed it perhaps more than anyone. It would also afford me some quiet time and a break from the guilt I felt watching Erin handle our daily lives on her own. I needed to spend some time alone.

Erin and the kids bustled out the door, calling out their goodbyes, overnight bags and electronics in tow. I closed the door behind them and felt a sense of relief. I could put to rest the brave face I wore for them, if only temporarily. As the sudden quiet blanketed the house, I hobbled over to my leather chair in the family room and gratefully collapsed into it. The pain in my legs flared as they relaxed, and I reclined back into my favorite position. It was always easy to melt into this chair as my skin rested against the cool leather.

My eyelids felt heavy, and my body badly wanted to drift off into sleep, but the unrelenting waves of hot pain emanating from my joints and traveling down my limbs made it impossible. The sun set slowly on this day, and the world transitioned from bright, warm sunshine into cold darkness.

I awoke the next morning to bright sunlight streaming in through the blinds. As I rubbed my eyes, it seemed the pain throughout my body had multiplied a hundredfold, perhaps most notably in my shoulders. I tried to stand up and couldn't. This could turn out badly. I was going to be here for four days. Did anyone even know I was here alone? I'm sure Erin must have told someone. A quick glance confirmed my cell phone was within reach; that was a good thing.

Erin called later that morning to check on me.

"How are you feeling?" she asked.

"Not too bad." I lied.

"How did you sleep last night?"

"Oh, I slept okay. The pain wasn't too bad." More lies. I quickly shifted the focus off me. "How are you guys doing? How are the kids? Are you having fun?" She hesitated a second before answering. She knew I was dodging her questions.

"We're fine. The kids are having fun. We are getting ready to head down to the beach in a bit. Are you sure you are okay? I asked my friend Toni to check in on you. She said she would bring you something to eat." We chuckled a bit at that. I loved Toni's cooking.

"Go have fun! Give the kids a hug for me. Love you."

"I love you too."

Toni did in fact stop by a few hours later with her famous rice balls. I could not get up to open the door for her when she knocked. Trying to sound casual, I called for her to come on in. Toni entered the room, and when she looked at me, I saw the concern flicker across her face. I must have been quite a sight. Normally a physically active, athletically built guy, I was feeling anything but that, and it must have shown.

"Johnny, how are you doing? Erin told me you weren't feeling well." I could tell Toni was curious about what was wrong with me. So was I.

"Yeah, Toni, I'm not doing too well right now. Not sure what's going on, we're thinking it may be Lyme disease. The doctor has got me on some antibiotics, so I should be doing better soon." She stayed for a little while, and we chatted a bit. I thanked her for stopping by and for the rice balls, of course. Little did she know they were the only thing I had energy to eat over those next four days. It was while eating them I noticed I was now having difficulty swallowing. *Terrific. I'll just add it to my list of mysterious ailments.*

I sat in that chair until my family came home. Getting up was so excruciating. I only attempted it when it became a necessity. Sitting for hours on end with nothing to interrupt the flow of my mind, I slipped into a trancelike state. Thoughts of what I should be doing, what I needed to be doing swirled through my mind, and I sat, unable to move.

I knew I was dying. It was an inexplicable knowing, a quiet fact. What would that mean for my family? How would they get by? What financial burdens was I leaving for them to contend with? I thought about the world without me in it. What had I contributed? I considered whether I had lived a good life. It made me think of Erin. She had a habit of cleaning up the house and tying up all the loose ends from the day, before retiring to bed each night. It was important to her that she put an end to each day when it was done and that she started each new day with a clean slate. My loose ends seemed to simply unravel and tangle themselves into the next day. That was no way to leave a life.

For days, I watched the world outside my window gradually take on form and shape as the sun rose in the sky each morning, and then I watched the world disappear again, swallowed by the darkness of nightfall. Light dispelled darkness, and darkness smothered the light over and over again in a vicious cycle. I prayed.

Before too long, I heard the familiar sound of the car pulling in the driveway, car doors slamming, and excited voices laughing and bickering and chatting away. The back door swung open, and suddenly the house was filled with the colors and sounds and energy of happy, tired, sun-kissed children and my beautiful, smiling, rosy-cheeked wife.

The children excitedly filled me in on their trip and all their beach adventures. Brittany showed me the shells she collected, and Kylie proudly showed me her new bright-pink Ocean City T-shirt. Johnny told me about the giant sandcastle he made and how the tide came in and washed it away. "We missed you, Dad." Seeing them laughing and happy again was exactly what I needed in that moment. Erin was studying me while the kids were talking. After a little while, she asked them to take their things upstairs so she could unpack them and wash their clothes.

"How are you feeling?" she asked, turning to me after the kids clamored upstairs. Her eyes were clouded with concern. I just shook my head. "You have a follow-up appointment this week. We should be getting the blood-test results." We both knew everything hinged on those results.

The day had arrived. My legs held out just long enough for me to collapse into the soft, padded armchair in the waiting room. Erin sat down next to me, and we both sighed. We were finally going to get some answers. She picked up a *People* magazine and absently started thumbing through it. My eyes darted to every movement in the office. It was a reflex I could not control and had been a source of distraction my entire life. Even on this day with so much hanging in the balance, the distractions were constant.

The nurse finally stepped into the waiting room and called my name. Erin and I both flinched. Our nerves were frayed. We followed the nurse to the sterile, harshly lit exam room. She asked us to have a seat and said the doctor would be in shortly. My heart was racing, my mouth dry. This was it. Erin and I exchanged a quick meaningful glance; she put her hand over mine and attempted a smile.

I jumped a bit when I heard the quick tap on the door and then the door opening as the doctor walked in. He looked somber, and my heart sank. He greeted us both and confirmed that the test results were in. The news was not what we wanted to hear. "I was hoping your tests would reveal more, but they were inconclusive. We do know, however, that this is not Lyme disease." *Inconclusive.*

I felt a burning lump form in my throat as we shared an uncomfortable stare. This highly respected doctor, an expert in his field, could not identify what was wrong with me. I had reached the end of the line. I knew I had just been handed a death sentence. My body was shutting down. I could feel it. It didn't matter what all these countless test results revealed or didn't reveal. My body was slowly failing. No one knew why; therefore, no one knew how to stop it. "If you find you're having difficulty breathing, go right to the hospital," he said.

"Okay," was the only word I spoke, and with that, Erin helped me up, and we hobbled out of the office together. I lacked muscle strength, and Erin had returned to her weary state. We were completely drained. It felt like I was on a plane that was crashing, and all I could do was haphazardly pray.

Erin was shaken. She drove us around in circles, too stunned to speak, until we ultimately ended up at a tiny Mexican restaurant. At first, we sat across from each other in silence, neither of us eating and neither quite sure what to say. Our minds were racing. Erin reached over and took my hand, consoling me. I felt a familiar sense of calm wash over me, as I always did when she touched me. I was immensely grateful, and through my mental anguish and physical pain, my heart warmed with love and admiration for her.

"They are going to be fine with you," I finally said. I was speaking of our children. "You are a wonderful mother, and I know you will do a great job raising them. They are so blessed to have you for their mother." She stared at me. Speaking about our children's future in this way was basically admitting to the fact that I might not make it through this. We had never really said this out loud to each other. Sitting in this tiny restaurant, oblivious to the other people present, we both wept. Our tears flowed as we grieved the long life we had planned to spend together and all the plans we had made and family milestones that we would not get to experience together. We cried for our children and how their worlds would be forever changed, and we cried because the pain of losing each other was simply too much to bear. Erin once again helped me to stand, and as always, she supported me as I moved unsteadily out to the car.

"We are going to have to let the kids know what is going on. We have to prepare them," Erin said quietly as we drove home. I nodded.

The fact that neither of us really knew what was going on did not help matters.

"How do we explain this to them without scaring them?" I wondered out loud.

"Well, they're already scared," she replied. "They can see what's happening, and I'm sure they can feel our tension. It may help to give them some answers. Sometimes not knowing is more frightening because the imagination takes over." I again nodded.

When we got home, Erin called Dea, who, being a nurse practitioner, was our local medical go-to person. We knew she would be able to offer some insight as to our next step. Erin briefly filled her in on this latest doctor's appointment. "I'm coming right over," she insisted.

Minutes later, Dea was entering the family room. She took one look at me and firmly said to Erin, "He needs to go to the hospital now." I hung my head in defeat.

Erin instantly responded, "No, we can't do it now. We have the kids, and we need to arrange for someone to take care of them. We'll go in the morning." She looked concerned but reluctantly agreed that it could wait until morning but no later.

Early the next morning, Erin and I sat down with the kids after breakfast. Dea was on her way to accompany us to the hospital, and we knew we had to let the children know what was going on. Erin arranged for a friend to come stay with the kids, so our time to talk with them was limited. The kids looked back and forth between us, puzzled. Erin took a deep breath and started.

"We wanted to talk with you a bit about Dad's condition." Their eyes grew a little bigger. "We went to the doctor yesterday, and they still don't know what's wrong with him. So we are going to the hospital to see some other doctors. Hopefully they will be able to tell us more. Okay?" The kids nodded slowly.

"Is Dad gonna be all right?" Brittany asked, her face tightening.

"We will know more soon. Okay, honey? But first we have to get him to the hospital."

Dea arrived a few minutes later. She was going to accompany us to ensure a smooth check-in. Another close friend of Erin arrived shortly after to stay with the kids for the day. We hugged the children goodbye, thanked our friend for coming over on such short notice, and embarked on the latest stressful leg of our journey.

I was dreading going to the emergency room. Every experience I ever had in an emergency room involved no less than four hours sitting in the waiting room before being seen. This time, however, things were much different. Thanks to Dea, as soon as my admission forms and insurance information were collected, I was wheeled back to a private room in the ER and helped into bed. The pain I was feeling by this point was searing through me, and it felt like I was lying on plywood. My joints were hot to the touch and so swollen that they were nearly unrecognizable. Erin sat close to me, holding my hand, both of us wearing now-familiar blank expressions. Dea stayed long enough to make sure we were settled, that we were receiving the attention we needed, and then got ready to make her exit. "I will be checking in with you soon, okay?" She reassured us as she left.

After about three hours, a young doctor entered the room. He stood over us and asked how I was doing. My only answer was, "Lousy." I then asked him if they had found anything yet. He paused a second or two.

"Right now, we are exploring several different possibilities. One of which is Lou Gehrig's disease or ALS. Your symptoms are similar." His words hung in the air. Frantically Erin reached for her phone to call Dea. I asked her to hang up the phone so we could let this sink in a minute.

"That's just not good," I spoke solemnly.

The doctor said they would let us know as soon as they knew more and left the room. As the door closed behind him, I turned to Erin, and we looked at each other in knowing silence for a long moment.

ALS did mean a steady, progressive decline in function, yet I would have time to say goodbye. This news was devastating. I felt panicked. I wasn't ready. Where had my time gone?

I'm not prepared to face God, I thought to myself. I contemplated this idea for a moment. What would it be like standing before Him in my moment of reckoning? *I would feel ashamed*, I decided. A quick mental scan of my life reminded me of the many mistakes I had made and the many loose ends I had yet to tie up. I glanced over at Erin, and she was lost in her own thoughts, presumably contemplating a life she never imagined for herself and our children—a life without me. I knew she was strong enough to handle anything that came her way, but I knew it must have been a terrifying idea. I couldn't imagine my life without her. She had become such an important part of me, the idea of living a life without her was unthinkable.

Erin and I sat and waited for news. I was painfully aware of every second that ticked by. That was the day I learned that when you stare death in the face, time seemed to stand still.

After what felt like an eternity, another doctor entered the room. He was a bit older than the doctor we spoke with earlier. "I have good news for you," he said. My heart skipped a beat. Those were words I was not expecting to hear.

"We believe we know what's happening now. Based on the results of your blood work, it appears you have polymyositis." That was a totally new word. "It is a treatable condition but not curable. It's a disease that causes inflammation and destruction of your muscles. It commonly affects your skeletal muscles which are responsible for helping you make movements such as walking, sitting, or standing. You have reached the point," he continued, "where your muscle movements have become inhibited, and simple tasks such as lifting an object or standing from a sitting position have become almost impossible. The exact causes are not known."

He went on to explain that polymyositis is an extremely rare autoimmune disease, and there was not a lot of information readily available about it. "We do know this disease triggers autoantibodies to be produced by your immune system, and for reasons not understood, these autoantibodies attack your healthy tissue. Without treatment, you will eventually lose all muscle function and will most likely not live longer than another month." My mind was racing.

I knew I was dying.

He explained other common symptoms associated with the disease including arthritis, difficulty swallowing or speaking, shortness of breath, and exhaustion. I recognized every one of those symptoms. I had been living with them for months. The mental and emotional relief I felt was immeasurable, but the realization that I had come so close to death was sobering. I was not out of the woods yet, but someone finally understood what I had been going through and offered a logical explanation for it.

Treatment options existed, and the doctor explained that they would begin with high doses of corticosteroids to disrupt my immune-system function. He further explained that my body has been fighting an internal battle, one muscle squaring up against another, and it was imperative that we stop that battle from continuing as quickly as possible. He also explained that the muscles could not be regenerated. Whatever damage they suffered would be permanent. Erin and I breathed matching sighs of relief as we exchanged hopeful glances.

I was admitted to the hospital, and the battle to save my life was quickly under way. I immediately started receiving an extremely high dose of prednisone intravenously, and several days of extensive testing procedures began.

I received a CT scan and an MRI, and I was put under a general anesthetic for an esophageal biopsy, a minor surgery performed on my throat where a tissue sample was obtained to aid in diagnosing the disease.

X-rays were taken, a breathing test was administered, and blood was drawn every four hours. A muscle biopsy was performed on my left thigh in order to confirm the type and progression of muscle damage I had sustained.

Within a few days I started physical therapy to combat my increasing weakness and immobility. I was wheeled to a different area of the hospital several times a day, and the staff bustled around me. I passively watched this whirlwind of activity surrounding me as I had become completely unable to move on my own. I found myself completely and totally dependent on others for my most basic needs, and I surrendered to the idea. I had no choice.

On the third morning in the hospital, I opened my eyes, and something was amiss. I blinked. What was different? The pain was gone. Gone. For the first time in over three months, I was completely pain-free. I smiled to myself. The relief was indescribable.

After seven days, I was finally able to shower, and a nurse helped me with the daunting task of getting me up onto my feet. I tentatively took the first step with the aid of a walker and was overwhelmed by how difficult it was. I was determined to do this on my own and assured the nurse I was able to. She let me know that everything was set up for my shower and that there were two pull cords should I need assistance. I cautiously began to move toward the bathroom as she looked on, concerned I would fall. Exhausted but with a sense of accomplishment, I finally made it and closed the door behind me.

I turned on the light and gasped. There was a stranger looking back at me from the mirror. *That can't be me.* I studied the withered man before me. Unrecognizable even to myself, I looked as if I had instantly aged about thirty years. I had lost layers of muscle, My skin was hanging in folds, clinging to my now-prominent bony frame. I took a deep breath and gazed back into those tired eyes. I thought to myself right then, *It's just so hard to die.* The vibrant and physical me was gone, my spirit broken. I couldn't avoid following the lines of my naked body; they were so foreign to me. I looked frail, tired, and weak and questioned my ability to continue. Discouraged, I looked away.

CHAPTER 4

BANISHED TO THE LAND OF WRONGDOINGS

TILL DEATH DO US part was an unimagined fate. I had fallen in love with someone, and now I was forced to go on without her. I was still in shock, reeling from this tragedy, and was selfishly absorbed in my own suffering.

Since my early childhood, I had been plagued with self-destructive thoughts. My fulfilling life with Erin seemed to have reversed some of that early programming, but now that she was gone, my old internal tapes were up and running again at full speed. In these first days following Erin's death, I found myself feeling like an insecure, frustrated child once again.

Interestingly, I was haunted most by memories from my early childhood. As I drifted through the days, thoughts and images flooded my mind, and I was hard pressed to stop them. I thought back to a day as a young boy when I had arrived home after school. My two older sisters Kathy and Sue were peeking at me while walking across the front lawn. After I saw them, they hurried inside.

"Ha! Ha! We locked you out!" they taunted through the glass of the storm door. Each of them wagged their tongues, stuck thumbs in their ears, and fluttered their fingers wildly. Frustrated, I took my clenched fist and punched the window, shattering the glass in their faces.

My faith had just suffered a similar blow, and only shattered fragments of it remained. How could God have taken Erin away from us? He knew what she meant to us, how much we loved and needed her.

Why would He be so cruel?

The kids and I faced our new life head-on. There was no other option really. Mornings were as chaotic as ever as I made sure all three kids were up and dressed in time to catch the bus to school. This was no easy feat considering most mornings my illness caused me so much pain and weakness; it was difficult to get myself out of bed.

We soon developed a morning routine that worked for us. Lying in my bed down the hall from their rooms, I would yell for them to get up. "I'm up, Dad!" would be the responses from Brittany and Kylie. I would then wait five minutes, listening for clues that they were truly out of bed and getting dressed. If I didn't hear the telltale signs of kids getting ready, I would drag myself out of bed and down the hall to bang on doors.

Most mornings they made it, and some they didn't. When they didn't, we all piled into the car, and I drove them to school, lecturing and scolding them the whole way. I drove them to the bus stop every morning, regardless, because I wanted to spend as much time with them as I could before they left for the day. I also needed to physically see them get on the bus safely each day.

As soon I returned home, out of view of my children, I would return to my inner world of torment and failure. Instinctively I clung to original moments where I knew that I had failed. These scenes from my childhood played over and over in my mind, but why?

I focused quite a bit on one event that took place in kindergarten. I had been playing happily alone, minding my own business, intently building a house with life-size cardboard blocks, when a boy from my class stepped in the way of my fun.

"Gimme that block!" he demanded, snatching it out of my hands. He challenged me with a combatant stare. I said nothing. Stepping forward with an angry thrusting motion, my hands found the square of his chest, and with one sudden thrust, he fell backward.

The expression on his face as he fell was one of complete and utter shock. My house swallowed him alive. My strong, sturdy house came tumbling down around him. I mean, he just disappeared. There I stood, feet firmly planted, glaring back, standing over the boy, and I had no idea who he was. All I knew was that he barged into my fun, it made me angry, and I immediately acted without thinking. Years later, the scene was playing over and over in my mind and I didn't know why.

My teacher Mrs. Mundy had been very upset with me. I had displayed a certain aggression that most kids our age hadn't seen before. Judging from the reactions of my classmates and teacher, I had clearly stepped outside the box of acceptable kindergarten behavior. When I calmed down enough to look around the classroom, I noticed my classmates' puzzled expressions. "Who is this boy?"

In their eyes, I may have appeared big and strong; inside I felt shamefully small. It was too late. I couldn't take it back, and now I had to accept the consequences of my impulsive actions. It would be the beginning of a long, stressful journey.

I became the boy no teacher wanted in their class. It was difficult for me to work with others, and I couldn't be left alone because my mind would wander. I had no sense of time or how to process it, and every second seemed to just pass right through me. Afflicted with ADHD, I was impulsive, unpredictable, and often unaware of my socially awkward behavior until it was too late. I struggled to make decisions, wasting so much time that I would panic, get angry, and give up altogether.

The frustrated reactions of teachers and peers reflected back to me a negative image of myself that became ingrained over time. I was a bad boy. I was not as smart as the other kids. I was different. Now, following my wife's death, this familiar sense of self-loathing and self-rejection had returned.

The house was unusually quiet without Erin. The fact that she was gone forever seemed unreal. Items around the house remained where she had left them. It was as if she was out running errands and would be returning any minute. The list of groceries she had written in her neat, pretty handwriting was hanging on the refrigerator right where she left it. Her glasses were on the end table where she had placed them after taking them off for what would turn out be the last time. I found myself expecting her to call me or come home at the times she normally did and felt the cold punch of reality every time I remembered she was gone forever. My phone would never again light up with a call from her, and she would never again walk through the back door with the rustle of shopping bags in tow. I was caught guilty of loving someone else much more than I ever loved myself. In way too deep, I now understood tangible fear as my broken walls so haphazardly tumbled down on me.

Though my children seemed to find comfort in the company of good friends, I felt the need to keep them close as they were all I had left of Erin. They were now solely my responsibility, and I felt overwhelmed by the knowledge that I must now raise our three children alone. *Alone.* That word echoed in my head, and I felt it deep in the pit of my stomach.

As I processed the realities of this new life, disturbing scenes from my childhood continued to intrude on my attempts to adjust.

Preparing dinner for the kids one night, I was suddenly besieged with a memory of tiptoeing past my best friend Johnny's house and the spot where he was hit by a car. I heard his desperate cries in my head. The sight of his mangled limb was terrifying, and my immediate reaction had been not to stop and help him or comfort him but to run home as fast as I could without looking back.

"Dad?" Brittany was staring at me from across the dinner table. "Dad, did you hear what I said?" Snapped back to reality, I looked up to see all three kids looking at me, perplexed. "I said I'm going to sleep at Emma's tonight. Okay?" Flustered, I nodded.

"Sure, honey. That's fine. Do you need a ride over?" I scrambled to regroup.

"Um...no, Dad, she lives three houses down. I've been walking to her house since I was five!" Kylie giggled.

"Oh, right. My bad." I tried to laugh it off.

Brittany smiled, shook her head, and took a bite of her bread. I looked at her for a long minute. My little girl was growing up so quickly, and she was handling all of this so well. She had her mother's inner strength and resolve, yet I was very concerned about her. Brittany had been the only one of our children to witness the events of that night. She had seen the paramedics working on her mother and had looked out her bedroom window as they wheeled Erin out to the ambulance on the gurney. I marveled at how she seemed to be so effectively processing all of this. My little girl was stronger than I was.

As the days went on one into the next, reality began to set in that every passing moment carried me further away from the last time I saw Erin. Every moment took me further away from her. My childhood days continued flashing before me.

I had memories of sitting as if glued to a classroom chair, feet bouncing and tapping uncontrollably off the floor while images of flying down a tree-lined street at hyperspeed raced through my mind. I would frantically cling to my desktop. This is how I experienced every day in school. I felt no control over my own body.

Every year, my teachers probably shuffled the deck in hopes they didn't get me in class. Surely, I was a card that they would have wanted to trade for anyone else. I became accustomed to my teachers losing their cool with me.

One teacher was pushed to the point of yelling, "I didn't become a teacher for this!" following one of my now-frequent classroom incidents.

During elementary school, it was decided that my desk would be separated from the rest of the class. Positioned up in front with my face only two feet from the blackboard, I had to look back over my shoulder to see my teacher. I was a daily spectacle.

Isolated from my classmates, I began to feel ostracized. They were all flourishing, interacting with, and receiving approval from teachers and the other students, but I was banished to the land of wrongdoings. It was hard for me to connect with teachers, so it was difficult to build a relationship and receive encouragement.

Feeling bored and disconnected, I entertained myself by tripping other children, wrestling boys, and bothering girls on the school bus. The laughs I received from my classmates only served to encourage this behavior. My young mind grew more distracted, and I became less able to control my actions. My mantra became "I didn't mean it!" I seemed to be constantly apologizing, yet I wasn't learning from my mistakes. There was no thought of consequences. I would push people until I saw the grinding of the teeth, a clenched fist shaken, or was even punched in my stomach, and only then would I realize I had pushed too far. I lived moment by moment, totally unaware that my time, like a stopwatch, was ticking away. As the kids around me learned faster, I continued to fall behind.

My report cards began to reflect the challenges I was facing, and processes were put in place and accommodations made to help me to stay on track. To help facilitate this, the support of my parents was sought. My mother did not react well to the feedback she received from my teachers. Their requests for at-home support with my schoolwork were met with hostility and defensiveness.

"I'd like to know what each of you are doing to help my son," she would respond through gritted teeth. "What exactly are you doing?" She felt no sense of responsibility for my academic success but rather saw my teachers' efforts as a criticism of her parenting.

My father's reaction was a bit more pragmatic.

"John, did you get your homework assignments signed by the teacher today?" he would sternly ask.

"No, I forgot," was my typical answer.

In first grade there was a desperate effort to put my excessive energy to use and to keep me out of trouble, I was assigned to help the janitor, Mr. Shulery, clean up the cafeteria after lunch. Every day, I was the only student who would stay behind after my classmates left, clearing trays and garbage left behind on the tables. I even got to use the giant push broom. My favorite distraction was taking the empty cardboard milk cartons found on the table, placing them on the floor, and stomping on them until they made a loud popping sound that was amplified by the empty cafeteria walls. Mr. Shulery would shake his head and laughingly remind me to stay on task.

"Dad, we got report cards today!" Brittany called out as she walked in the back door after school. She swung her giant backpack onto the kitchen table and started rummaging through its contents. "I got mostly Bs and two As!"

"That's great, honey! Good job!" It was amazing to see how well the kids were melding right back into their school life. I was relieved they weren't faced with the same academic struggles I had, yet I was all too aware of the other massive challenges they were now facing that I never had to contend with. The loss of a mother was a devastating blow, yet our children were pushing through.

Early childhood memories continued to invade my thoughts. Suddenly I was about seven, and my father had taken me hunting early one crisp fall morning. We walked deep into the woods, and being a man who preferred to do things on his own, my father sat me on a rock and told me not to move until he got back. I sat there very restless, wearing a bright-orange vest, and waited for him.

As time passed slowly, the trees took on sinister forms and shapes, and cold fear began to creep in. I heard strange noises. I imagined the creatures that were making those sounds. I wanted to go home. My body began to tremble in fright. I could not sit there anymore simply awaiting my fate.

I started walking in the direction I believed would lead me back to the car. I was wrong. The farther I walked, the more those sinister shapes and sounds seemed to engulf me, and the car was nowhere in sight. I was walking in circles. I was lost. Total panic set in. No one knew where I was. How would they find me? I began to cry. My tears blurred my vision and made it that much harder for me to see the path in front of me. I began to cry out in fear. I came upon a valley, and as I looked down at it through my tears, I saw my father walk out of the brush, and I began screaming. He looked flustered as he had heard my cries, and no doubt he thought I had been hurt. Relief washed over me as I saw him turn to walk toward me. I was going home.

As a kid, I used to blow off steam by throwing stones. I was obsessed. I cradled piles of rocks in my shirt and often threw them for hours. I threw them at my friends too. We all seemed to have fun with it. I developed amazing precision, with long distances and moving targets being my specialty.

One day while throwing stones with some of my neighborhood buddies, I caught a friend off his game. He stood about a hundred feet away from me. I found a perfectly shaped flat rock, and accounting for wind, velocity, and distance, I hurled it with precision through the air. I watched as it banked at just the right angle and headed straight for my unsuspecting mark. He never saw it coming. My stealthy projectile struck him on the side of his head, and a split second later, he collapsed in a heap to the ground.

I turned to my cohort, mouth gaping in astonished pride.

"Oh my god! Did you see that?" I exclaimed in amazement.

"You nailed him!" My buddy laughed, holding up his hand for a high five. I slapped it hard, celebrating my victory. I turned to see Dave in the distance rolling on the ground. His brother Pat stood over him, offering a helping hand. Unfazed by our friend's suffering, our chants and laughter filled that summer day. Ironically, I now found myself knocked to the ground by an unexpected, painful blow.

When I was about ten, I also loved playing baseball but only when things went my way. I was small for my age, and center field was my position because it always kept me moving.

There was one moment that stayed with me, and I could see it in my mind's eye like it happened yesterday. I was playing in a Little League game at the field in front of our town's elementary school. Parents and kids looked on from the hillside behind the field.

There was a hit up the middle, and I was playing deep. The ball bounced erratically toward me, giving me too much time to think. Hesitating, I timidly placed my glove near the ground, but the ball skipped between my feet and headed for the wall behind me. In disbelief, I chased it down like my life depended on it. Nearing the center-field wall, however, I knew the play was over. My efforts became worthless.

I was enraged, and all I could think of as I ran toward that now-useless ball was that I was going to throw it as hard as I could away from me. The motions of that moment were supernatural. During those next few seconds, as the ball of my failure streaked through the sky, time suddenly seemed to move slowly. I knew I had caused this feeling. I had slowed down time itself. For one fleeting moment, I felt in control of something.

Everyone watched as the ball reached its peak altitude and charted its course, heading straight for the families who were there to cheer us on. My monstrous hurl sent the ball careening off a thirty-foot hill that towered behind home plate. I had thrown this now-dead ball back across the entire field, literally right out of the park.

My fleeting sense of control was replaced by an incredibly intense, rip-my-face-off anger. I began pacing erratically back and forth, berating myself. I had let my friends down. I had failed my teammates. My rage was directed entirely inward. Gradually I became aware that people were watching me. My error and subsequent fit of anger were on display for all to see, as vibrant as the red on my uniform. I found myself, once again, as the center of undesired attention. It took an unusually long time to calm myself down. I dreaded returning to the bench after the inning. I knew my teammates were going to give me a hard time about my ridiculous mistake.

To my surprise, as I warily approached the bench, my teammates spotted me and cheered, jumping to their feet. They ran over, hugging me, patting me on the back and laughing. They were all calling out their praises, declaring my biggest mishap to be the best play they had ever seen. I was speechless.

"Holy crap! How did you do that? You threw the ball out of the park!"

"Dude, you almost took out my mom!"

"That was awesome!"

It was strange to realize that what I considered to be my greatest flaws were being met with such admiration and praise. I was confused.

"Hey, Dad! Are you driving me to cheer practice?" I was jolted back to the present by Erin standing before me, dressed in her pink and black cheerleading uniform. I blinked, startled, and Kylie's face came into focus. Her long, blonde hair, so much like her mother's, was pulled back smoothly into a sleek, high ponytail with what I affectionately referred to as her *Pretty Poof.*

To create the *pretty poof,* the hair in front was carefully puffed up a bit on top and then blended in with the rest of her hair. Kylie was very particular about her poof, and tonight's creation was exceptional. I smiled.

"Wow! That's one heck of a poof you got going on there, Ky!" Kylie grinned back at me with her pink braces. "Thanks! Are you driving me? I have to be there in fifteen minutes."

"Yes, let me find my keys." Sometimes it seemed that life was continuing as if nothing had changed, except everything had changed. My best friend died.

My thoughts drifted to the day my very first friend Johnny moved away. The morning he was leaving, I stopped by on my way to school to say goodbye.

Johnny and his family were leaving before the movers were scheduled to follow with their belongings, so the house was still cluttered with boxes and furniture. As the family bustled around, making sure they had what they needed for their road trip to their new home, I sat down on the edge of a chair in the family room, tears rolling down my cheeks. I didn't know what I was going to do without him. We saw each other every day. We played together, challenged each other, and told each other our most important secrets.

Johnny never judged me; he accepted me for who I was. It was hard to imagine he would be gone forever. I followed Johnny and his family outside and watched them all piled into their shiny, red Honda. The car backed out of the driveway, and I walked alongside as Johnny and I called out our goodbyes through the rear window.

"Bye, everybody, drive carefully!" I called after them, waving.

"See ya, buddy!" Johnny called back. Our cheerful, nonchalant parting belied what I was feeling. As I watched their car drive away, I continued waving to them with one hand and wiped my now freely flowing tears with the other. I was late to school that day, and I didn't care. My best friend was gone.

CHAPTER 5

MY BROKEN WALLS

"HOW ARE YOU DOING, John? How do you feel?" These two questions I now fielded from everyone I knew. I unthinkingly responded with the easiest answer I assumed everyone would appreciate hearing, "I am okay." But I knew differently. My core thoughts just were not behaving.

The truth was, despair was eating my insides away, and I couldn't begin to formulate that answer in words. There was one thing I knew for certain: I would always bear this sadness after losing the part of me that I loved the most. Erin had simply vanished, and I was left to roam through the rooms of our home and my life aimlessly, misguided and hollow inside. How had I allowed myself to become so dependent on another that I would ever feel this empty, so godforsaken without them?

It was another new morning, and I now knew what it meant to grieve. My ravaged body was weak, and my resolve was even weaker. My illness left me physically vulnerable, and I instinctively insulated myself from the outside world, resulting in a heightened sense of isolation.

I had lost my love forever. I pushed away these heavy thoughts and tried to adjust to this newfound loneliness. All this compression that should surely lead to depression only helped conceal the evidence of my symptoms.

Who am I? Am I a martyr? A martyr for the gift of life?

I was losing the ability to control my thoughts and emotions.

"Oh God, I need to stop this train. I want to get off."

This emotional express was too much for one, but it wouldn't stop for simply me.

Good memories were drying up as my world turned parched and desolate. I convinced myself there was no one to talk to, no one who would understand, and there was no one who could help. Storm clouds lurked overhead, and eternity poked at me from the darkness. At a pace that couldn't continue, time was unwinding on me again at lightning speed, and I couldn't keep up. The second hand continued to strike my very soul, inflicting unfathomable wounds. I was unable to find happiness. I couldn't admit to sadness, and madness struck my core deep, deep inside.

Everyone around me was on notice. I simply did not have the mental or emotional capacity to consider other vantage points or motives. I simply retreated from potential conflict, rendering guilt before assuming innocence. It was part of my self-protective insulation. I had reached my limit. *God, I can't do this. How would you do it? Please show me how.* These pleas rang out in my head but seemed to fall on deaf ears. I was pushing away my support system, my true confidants. *Or had they left me?* I became a fixture in this dark illusion, and if I stayed here too long, I could lose my mind.

Erin had passed through to the kingdom of heaven, and I lay here, the despondent prisoner chained to these rusty gates of hell. I struggled with what I felt was deserved, so I nursed these sickening feelings and sought out this isolation, convincing myself it was my safe place. Speculating on my chances to survive, this became just a roll of two dice. *Oh no, its snake eyes and the temptation to succumb is circling me.*

At some point in all our lives, whether we deny our pain or feel it is deserved, we find ourselves stranded in this desolate place. We wander here in this lonely realm, trapped inside what troubles us. Some of us impose our anguish and hopelessness on others with morbid hopes of enlisting them.

Stay close. Follow me, everyone, or get burned. This is no place to stay for long.

Unable to compose myself, I reverted to my childlike impulses. I was that babe lost in the woods again, crying my way down a river of dreams. I accessed these images quickly and with ease as all these moments boiled back to the surface. I wandered without purpose, reveling among troubling thoughts, stripped of instincts to survive.

As time passed, my shocked numbness began to lift, and I felt the full weight of my walls that had crumbled down on me. I now felt the fear I had seen in the face of that boy I pushed down in my kindergarten class. Just as he knocked down my walls so many years ago, my adult fortification had now tumbled but this time I was the one who was buried.

Erin's life was startlingly erased, and I was left alone to stare at my own. Self-absorbed and fragile, I felt the same anger as I had when that little boy took my block. On that day, my teacher disciplined me by making me sit alone in the classroom while my classmates enjoyed recess, running and playing outside in the fresh air and sunshine.

I remembered sitting alone and feeling the gloominess of the empty classroom containing me like a jail cell. Once again, I felt alone and trapped and forced into solitary confinement, this time by my own thoughts. The sense of rejection and isolation that had been introduced into my world on that day continued to thrive within me now, as an adult.

The disturbing flashbacks continued.

There were those crooked basement stairs. I had been retrieving a large can of Hi-C for my father, and while attempting to navigate the uneven stairs, I tripped over the top step. Falling forward into the kitchen, I dropped the heavy juice, shearing off half of my little finger. I cried in horror as I lifted my bloodied, trembling hand, seeing a gash that exposed my bone. Looking frantically about, I carried on violently shaking.

Next, the screech of those tires and the roar of young Johnny's desperate cry as I ran over to him. My neighborhood friend was surrounded by strangers, but I could see him through the crowd lying there at the edge of the road, crying out. He was clutching his bloody leg, and I saw his protruding bones. Frightened, I turned and ran home.

Reliving these painful images brought me closer to my own current pain. As disturbing as the memories were, I studied each of them carefully, noting the important connections between the past and the present.

I sat at my desk in the front of the classroom, and as the teacher talked to the rest of class, I dipped my finger in the chalk dust and painted happy, smiling faces on the blackboard. Some children giggled. Encouraged, I drew more faces resulting in more laughter. I was always left with a finger full of dust. These smiling faces I drew were masks that covered how I really felt—hurt. As I drew them, my mind wandered to an unknown place far removed from this world.

"John Whitmeyer! Are you listening?" I flinched as my teacher's sudden high-pitched shrill jolted me back to earth. Eyes cast downward, I turned away from the smiling masks I was drawing and faced my shame.

Like that dizzying, old feeling at my desk, the trees were flying past me once again as my train throttled up right down memory lane. I immersed myself in the deluge of negative feelings that were crushing me.

I saw my most regrettable moments over and over. I grappled with the pain that was once again screaming out of my young body. I saw my unfeeling disregard for a friend after I stoned him to the ground. That ball, I can't ever forget that ball that rolled to the wall. I had been the weakest link. *Why couldn't I make that play?* My thoughts were self-absorbed and childish. I knew that. During this time, however, I felt like that child again. I was my own worst enemy, a decorated marksman, well trained in the art of malicious self-persecution. Life had troubled me.

God, I must have earned this agony.

I kept seeing my classmates laughing, not with me, but at me. The whispers of ridicule surrounded me like thieves secretly stealing my innocence. My peers stared at me, and now I finally saw their unsmiling faces for what they were—hostile and judgmental. I had always been too distracted to notice or care. It was a dangerous deficiency thinking I was the funny one. I sensed their disgust. I was in contempt, offering no defense. I felt like the outsider once again among my peers, so shrewdly exiled in this trial by jury, displaced on the fringe of society, I saw myself as the forgotten one.

I remembered all these feelings vividly. My body ached and stung as I stared off into the abyss, unable to sleep. Over the course of my life, pain had been served up in various flavors, and I sampled all of them. I felt resentful. Why did illness choose me? It was unfair. People told me I looked fine. Well, I wasn't. I didn't have it together, not by a long shot. I was fragmented and suffering. Internal chaos abounded. Battered and bruised, I continued to seek out that child within me, perhaps because he was all that remained of my meager identity.

How am I supposed to guide my children through this when I feel like a lost child myself?

My heart was broken for Erin's innocent life. She was so precious, such an important, vital force in my life yet was just simply gone in the blink of an eye. Why? Was her life not meaningful enough? If her life wasn't meaningful enough, what on earth was? I struggled here in this vacuum, pinned to these thoughts.

When people popped in to check on us, I tried not to reveal my confusion to them, but it was almost impossible not to. How was I to play this new hand I had been dealt? *How should I behave?* Lying about my true feelings seemed deceitful, but I couldn't impose my delusions on those around me. I locked my corrosive feelings inside where they festered as I wore a smiley face mask. The corrosion within me was beginning to have physical repercussions. This body of mine grew weaker by the day. All these feelings, old and new, inflicted a living, growing pain that threatened to engulf me.

As I suspected, my illness was flaring again, and a full-blown relapse seemed imminent. I didn't want to end up in the hospital again. This destructive disease was forcing my body to wage a battle against itself again, and the burning pain indicated my muscles and joints were taking heavy fire. Self-pity paved the way for self-destruction. My own negative thoughts and emotions had reignited my autoimmune disease. I was literally destroying myself on both the emotional and physical level. Contemplating surrender, I ran frantically with no cover on the receiving end of a deadly barrage.

The degree of war depended on where I placed myself, and without strength or strategy, I became fixed on my retreat. I just didn't see how I could achieve a victory.

Erin, you were just lying there, and I knelt before you. Why couldn't I react more quickly? Just as your body was locked up tightly, I, too, froze in fright. Why didn't you answer me? We were breathing together, but you couldn't breathe on your own. The 911 operator on the phone told me to move you to the floor. But I was too weak, and this weakness now swallows me. Did I even compress correctly?

I was thinking *no* as these horrible seconds moved in repetition, replaying over and over. In my own mind, I was the primary suspect.

Turbulent winds with violent tunnels forcefully stripped away all the things that shielded me.

"My God, what have I done?" I said it again and again with no real answer. The person I had lived for died at my hands. I had felt the weight of Erin's soul skip right through my fingers. This was it for me; it was this scene that broke me. It ripped me open to my very core. I couldn't remember watching something with more pure horror.

Erin, I'm sorry I couldn't save you.

Pushed on by opposing forces battling for my very soul, I teetered along a jagged edge. I could see down in front of me and knew I must be looking at hell.

In that moment of silence, my mind flooded with a spectrum of emotions as I fearfully dared to stare down my own in-between. On the precipice of my fate, I was tortured with misery and defeat and felt my long battle was lost.

I questioned my significance; perhaps no one would even miss me if I were to join Erin. I finally had enough of living in this body that had been so harshly controlling me for as long as I could remember. I couldn't bear another moment alone with myself. I knew the decision to live or die was mine alone to make, so I began to obsess over my options.

I'm dying anyway.

I was also aware that the trauma of recent events was taking a physical toll on me, killing me faster.

What if I just helped that process along?

There was one thing I knew for sure now, and that was dying was easy. I was there with Erin on her last night. I saw just how easy it could be to suddenly disappear.

I began to feel a sense of urgency from the dark, oppressive forces within me. It felt as if there was a battle underway for ultimate ownership. I was feeling pressured to act quickly to just put an end to the agony once and for all. As that familiar train accelerated, I braced myself for another dizzying ride. Any tree flying by, any impulsive thought, if it occurred at just the right time with just the right amount of pain and despair, could very well be the death of me. Simply turning into one of those trees, giving in to one of those thoughts could put an end to this madness right now. I was well past the point of feeling lost and alone. I was about to put an end to me.

As I contemplated facilitating my own end, I realized my final decision hinged on how I would feel the moment I went as I lay chained to this hell that contained me. A horrifying thought struck me.

What if I end my life here on earth only to find myself stuck in this very moment of despair for eternity?

I imagined the painful memories and fearful, angry words continuing to tear at me forever and being unable to right my wrongs.

I have that opportunity now. I could do the hard work.

I knew these were powerfully dark forces I was dealing with, and I was reassured that they were eagerly watching and anxiously waiting to overwhelm me.

I had been stuck all along, spinning round and round, caught in an emotional revolving door. I knew my last go-round would become the moment I would live in for all of eternity. If I allowed a death wish to play on through, I would die without resolution and therefore be thrust into this dark moment forever. I would be forever embracing the origins of my distressing thoughts, each one tagged with troubled emotions that continue lashing out over and over.

With that epiphany, I knew what my final decision had to be. I had to live. The energy within me shifted slightly. It felt lighter, purposeful, and I felt a twinge of something I hadn't felt in a very long time—hope.

Could all this upset heal me?

I committed to focusing all my available energy on the monumental task of staying alive and as well, seizing the opportunity that I only just realized had always been available to me—the opportunity to work on myself. I knew the road would not be easy, and I was fearful. I wasn't hopeful of holding it together well. Desperately, I clung to my precious life, seeing myself as a sacrifice, disavowed to ever die in peace.

CHAPTER 6

THIS IS HIM

SOMETHING INSIDE KEPT TUGGING at me, pulling me back from the edge of the dark abyss. As much as I wanted to lie in bed and cry like a newborn baby, I had three little people depending on me, three little people that just lost their mother and who were dealing with their own individual grief.

I watched each of them move through their days, waiting for one of them to break down. They never did, at least not in front of me. It was worrisome, quite frankly. Aside from Kylie missing the cheerleading competition that took place a week after Erin's death, my children resumed their activities and social calendars as if nothing had happened. I noticed they approached all of it with stone faces, and there was an uptick of infighting among them. My method for dealing with that was to encourage them to talk and not fight.

"Go to your room and scream. Go cry. Go hit your pillow. Get it out. You are all hurting. No one's pain is greater or more important than anyone else's." This was a common discussion in our house, and the slamming of bedroom doors became the soundtrack to our lives. I knew the pitfalls of bottling up emotions and thoughts; eventually they would make themselves known and most likely not before the physical damage was done. I understood the importance of facing these dark thoughts and feelings head-on. I was just not very good at it.

Not wanting to be a burden, I rarely asked anyone for help with the overwhelming responsibilities I now faced alone. My illness rendered me unable to work, so I threw myself into caring for my kids. I was anxious to shuttle them to cheerleading practice, friend's houses, softball, whatever they needed to carry them through this time. My body and mind were weary, but I was grateful to have a sense of purpose, and what greater purpose could there be than to take care of our children?

Through it all, running in the background of every minute of every day, I missed Erin, and I wanted to be with her. This now defined me. My heavy heart was broken.

One gray afternoon about a month after Erin passed away, I was sitting with Johnny on the couch in the family room. We were sitting in the same spot where I had last spoken with Erin. Johnny had flopped over onto his side head-on the cushion and was quietly staring off into the distance. I wondered if he was looking for his mother. I gazed at him for a long moment, taking in the features of his innocent, little boy face. He had such beautiful blue eyes; they were just like his mother's. *He's only eight.* How unfair that he had been forced to deal with such a tragic loss. I imagined how his idea of life had been forever altered, how the unexpected loss of his mother at such a tender, young age would impact him. I was sure his faith had been shattered. Our feelings were probably very similar, yet I was supposed to be leading the way for him, guiding him, and helping him through all of this pain. In that moment, I felt the overwhelming weight of responsibility that rested on me. It was crucial that I find the strength to do this for my children.

I held Johnny closer to me and couldn't help but think about Erin. I left her to go to bed just weeks before as she sat in this very spot. I could envision her entering the room at any moment. It would have been such a natural sight. Her warm presence was strong all around us. I wondered if Johnny was feeling her. I wondered if she could feel us too.

Was that how it worked? I wondered. *If we can still feel her around us, can she still feel us?* No one really knew the answer to that, did they?

After sitting for a moment in that blissful silence, something unseen struck me with a jolt and electrifying chills shot through me like a bolt of lightning. I instinctively looked back over my right shoulder for the source. I could see nothing, but I immediately felt an unmistakably powerful, commanding presence. It made no logical sense, of course, but with words unspoken, a silent knowing grew with in me. It was Him. There were no adequate words to describe such magnificent strength of such a divine presence. I knew it could only be my God.

A powerful thought formed in my mind, only it was not mine. I knew it was not of this world but was coming from somewhere inside me and all around me at the same time. There was no voice, but I could hear Him with perfect clarity. "Feel through Me." The meaning of those three words and the pure energy that accompanied them was instantly known to me and was so powerful, so intense that I instinctively bowed my head.

Those three words immediately instilled within me physical order and moral order and the strength to face anything. I could not see Him, but once again I simply knew. He could be experienced anywhere by any of the senses. This is Him.

I was being called to see myself the way He saw me—through the eyes of a parent. I felt His compassion, His unconditional love, and His faith in me that I could accomplish anything. In that moment, I had a crystal-clear vision of how He saw me and how severely distorted and inaccurate my own self-image really was. I knew that if I could learn to see myself through God's eyes, to know myself as He knew me, I would be led out from under the dark turmoil that had been threatening to engulf me. In an instant, I could see the profound ripple effects this change in outlook and approach would have on not only my life but on the lives of my children and all the lives that my life touched.

I knew this undertaking would be challenging, even painful at times, yet there was simply no turning down His personal invitation. No transformation came easily. The caterpillar would suffer tremendously before emerging as the more breathtaking version of itself—the butterfly.

This process would require me to look at myself and my life with compassion. I would have to forgive myself for my transgressions while at the same time learning from them so as not to repeat them. I also understood that I must allow myself to feel joy as well as pain to maintain a natural balance. I must let both emanate from me equally in a just fashion.

If I entered into this agreement with Him, making these changes within myself, I might become an example for others, most importantly my children, that they might also be inspired to see themselves through His eyes. Through these offerings of good faith, I knew I would find inner peace. I would need to trust in Him to lead me during my moments of weakness.

I'll position myself to move closer to Him. This was my path, and it was clearly paved before me. This was Him.

My senses became heightened, my perspective clearer. In that seminal moment, I was overcome with the call to act. I envisioned myself as an explorer now, searching for my elusive inner peace in a new world. I knew just where to begin looking.

CHAPTER 7

ARE YOU REAL?

THE FIRST TIME I heard about this special girl Erin was through my friend Tom as we began our first year in college. He had passed her on campus one day, and in his overly dramatic fashion, he tried to explain the encounter.

"Oh my god! You should have seen her!" He was grabbing at his hair and scratching his face like a lunatic. "She's gorgeous!" Our friends and I sat there puzzled, watching this bizarre display. I could only wonder, *Was this girl for real?*

Having never witnessed someone react to a girl the way Tom did, I knew I had to see her for myself. I was curious. Apparently, The Girl had moved into our dorm just two floors above us. Like the shy, inexperienced schoolboy I was, I quietly went out of my way to sneak a peek at her.

Late one afternoon, I was standing at the end of a long, well-lit hallway, and suddenly there she was. I spotted her at the far end, popping in and out of each room, laughing and talking. I only caught a quick glimpse of her, but it was enough to keep me thinking about her over the next few days. I thought about her bouncy curls, how perfectly her stylish outfit hung on her attractive frame, and her spunkiness. I was intrigued.

A day or two later, I was hanging out in my friend's room just killing time, when the door burst open and I suddenly found myself face to face with the beautiful girl with the bouncy curls. She grinned and tossed her head, using those curls to her advantage. "There's a party on the fifth floor," she called out. "And you're all invited." She paused a second, her startling blue eyes locked right in on mine, and she added, "You, too, John." I was stunned and a little embarrassed.

She knew my name. How did she know my name? We'd never met. She disappeared as quickly as she had appeared, but she left quite an impression. My friend and I didn't go to the party, but this girl with a sweet face framed in curls and a bubbly spirit had piqued my interest. Over the next few days, my mind would often wander back to that personal invitation and those curls. I was certainly intrigued.

The next day was Super Bowl Sunday. A group of us had gathered in the lounge to watch the game when a food fight broke out. Since I enjoyed throwing things and I was good at it, I was in my glory.

It happened so quickly. I reached down to pick something up, and half an orange hit me in the eye. Looking up in the direction from which it came, there she stood. Our eyes met momentarily as she stood in her perfect follow-through position. Her intended target was clear. As the juice began to burn my eye, I was forced to retreat and duck for cover. Using my shirt to wipe my face, I noticed she quickly went about her business picking others off. Though it appeared she had planned an attack on me, she quickly changed gears and kept moving.

No pun intended, but she really caught my eye. For some reason, I liked that she kept moving. It made her even more intriguing. The Super Bowl game soon drew everyone's attention, yet I couldn't focus on anything but her. I found myself searching for her in the crowd. She captivated me, and I quickly realized how difficult she was to catch alone. Like me, she seemed to be constantly moving.

At one point, I gathered my courage and seized an opportunity to sit down next to her. I extended my index finger, touching her thigh to make sure she was real. Something about this touch electrified me. Through touching Erin, I felt something powerful, something inexplicable.

My intrusive advance was met with an aggressive smack, but her glowing smile contradicted it. Again, completely out of character,

72

I extended my finger and lightly touched her, resting my finger a moment or two longer. "Why are you doing that? You're weird!" she exclaimed. I laughed quietly. On my third and final touch, I was a believer. I certainly felt something real. I had never done anything like that before, but I just knew I had to do something.

"You've got quite an arm there," I said finally. "My eye still hurts."

"Well, you asked for it," she teased, standing up.

"Where are you going? We just started talking!" I laughed.

"I only talked to you so you would stop touching me!" With that, she turned on her heel and walked away, infamous curls bouncing. I laughed harder. This girl had style.

Over the next several weeks, I found myself scanning the hallways for her as I walked around campus. We both had class at the same time in the same building, and if I could catch a quick glance of my new fascination, I was happy. One time we passed each other outside her classroom. As she got closer to me and made eye contact, I felt shy but still managed to quietly murmur a *hi*. Her cheeks grew ever so slightly pink.

"Where did you come from? Are you a ghost or something?" She laughed it off as she kept walking. I was hooked.

We had mutual friends, so we started seeing each other more frequently. The playful banter continued, yet I instinctively knew to tread carefully. Ever teasing and flirtatious, she naturally received a lot of attention from guys, and I took notice but tried not to let my insecurity show.

Whenever the opportunity presented itself, I would try to strike up casual conversation with her. These little exchanges provided clues about this elusive girl that made me want to know more. I found out she was a freshman. She was from a town about forty-five minutes from where I grew up. She had recently broken up with someone from home and wasn't quite over it.

Her reactions to me were my gauge, and I plotted my course accordingly. When I got too close, she let me know it right away.

"I'm not interested."

"Go date her. She likes you."

She made me laugh.

This girl had me off kilter. I sensed a strong attraction between us; it was palpable. At times I wondered if people around us could feel the electricity we gave off when we stood close to one another. Those electric moments didn't ever last long. Just as quickly and intensely as they came on, she would dance off, calling back a snarky remark over her shoulder. It was going to take time and patience to win this girl over, and there was not a doubt in my mind that she was worth the wait.

An interesting change began to manifest within me during this time. My posture straightened a bit in Erin's presence, and I began to enjoy the pressures of being a better person. I began to take notice of other people around me, more so than where the next party would be. As fun loving and rambunctious as she was, Erin made it clear that she liked me but had solid boundaries.

Through her actions and reactions, she conveyed a certain level of expectation, and it was clear she was not going to settle for less. I wanted very much to live up to her standard. Being held accountable and responsible for my actions somehow provided me with a new sense of empowerment. I began to treat people around me with more respect. It was as if I was waking up from a long slumber.

My excitement had to be met with tempered enthusiasm. I was unsure from one day to the next whether there was hope for me in Erin's life. She was strong and independent, and she reminded me of that every day.

"I'm not dating anyone! I'm finally free. I want to have fun!" she'd yell while dancing with her friends. Erin loved to dance. Tabletops, chairs, dorm-room beds—any surface was the perfect dance floor if the right song was on. When she was dancing, Erin was totally uninhibited, and I was amazed by how the energy in the room changed. All eyes were fixed admiringly on her. I preferred a more low-profile kind of existence; so for me, this was at once intimidating and intriguing.

As the semester began to draw to a close, a big year-end party was planned with all our friends, and I was excited as always to spend time with Erin. I felt this evening was going to be very important for us. The school year was ending. We were all going home for the summer, and it seemed if I had any real chance with Erin, we were going to have some kind of a breakthrough tonight.

Erin was distant with me at first. She barely said *hi* and was preoccupied with other partygoers for the first part of the evening. My heart sank a bit as my old familiar friend, doubt, began to creep in. Maybe I had misread her signals. Those signals of hers were so unpredictable and erratic; who could blame me? I tried not to let my disappointment show.

After a couple of drinks and some dancing, Erin began to warm up to me. At one point she came over to me and sat right down on my lap. I knew I had to be the happiest person in the room.

As the night wore on and the drinks flowed, Erin and I found ourselves alone in an empty bedroom. I leaned in for the kiss I had been planning since the moment I saw her. My heart raced.

The kiss was soft and sensual at first, filled with tender emotion, and then quickly became more intense as that electricity I felt between us quickly ignited into passion. I was completely swept away in my senses.

"Back off!" she abruptly yelled, shoving me away. She stood angrily with her hands up in front of her as if to block me. I stood frozen. I was stunned and confused. Erin had rattled my cage. Heck, she had knocked it off the table, sending my emotions into a free fall. Apparently, the train to heaven was only carrying one passenger— me. In the moment of our brief kiss, I had completely loved someone. The feeling did not appear to be reciprocated. I turned and left the room without a word.

I had worked diligently to prove myself without pressing too hard. She wasn't ready. Composing myself, I moved through the situation with dignity, still trying to be worthy of her respect.

After the semester ended, I watched out the window of my dorm room as Erin hopped in her car and simply sped off toward home. She never even said goodbye. I was crushed. I knew then I had fallen in love, and the idea that I wouldn't be seeing her for several months now left me feeling cold and empty. *How could she just leave like that?* Part of me was angry with her, and part of me really admired her ability to just drive away and not look back. Beneath the crushing waves of disappointment and self-doubt I was feeling inside, there was a calm, quiet, inexplicable knowing. I simply knew she had feelings for me and that she was just not ready to act on them. I knew this, and I knew I had to let her go for now. With this realization and sense of determination, I was already becoming a stronger man for knowing her. I would play this game with her for as long as it took to gain her trust and her love. But I was no doormat.

About a month after returning home from school, I decided to pay her a visit at her summer job. I hadn't heard from her at all, and I wasn't letting her off the hook that easily. I drove the forty-five minutes to the women's clothing store where she worked, and as I walked across the parking lot to the entrance, I reached up and snapped a dead twig from a tree as I passed.

I entered the store and spotted her blonde curls right away. She was standing behind the cash register and was clearly busy, a line of customers stretched around the counter. Clutching the dead twig, I took my place in line and waited for her to notice me. When there were only about two customers remaining ahead of me, she spotted me, and I saw her freeze for the briefest of seconds. Her slight reaction would have been imperceptible to anyone else, but I caught it. I also noticed the bright-pink flush start to creep upward from her neckline. Within a few seconds, her face was about two shades brighter than the soft-pink top she was wearing.

She continued ringing up the remaining customers in front of me. I could tell she was moving a little more stiffly than usual, her smile a little more forced. No one noticed but me.

When it was finally my turn, I stepped up to the counter in front of her. She looked at me and nonchalantly said, "Oh, hi. What are you doing here?"

"Oh, just passing through." I shrugged. "Thought I'd stop by and say hi since you just left school without saying goodbye and all." She stammered for a minute, not sure what to say. It was the first time I had the upper hand in this dance of ours, and I was enjoying myself. "Oh, I brought this for you, thought you might like it." I handed her the bent twig.

She stared at it and turned it over in her hand, puzzled. Rolling her eyes, she immediately tossed it in the trash can behind the counter. "You're an idiot."

"Well, I'm an idiot who got himself a new car and a new job. So there's that." Her blue eyes widened a bit at that news.

"Oh, that's great. Good for you! I'm having a great summer so far, lots of parties, lots of fun."

"Good for you," I said sincerely. "Well, I've got to get going. It was good to see you. Have a great summer. Maybe I'll see you around." I tried to strike the perfect balance between appearing unaffected and well intentioned. With that, I turned and walked out, palms sweaty, head held high. I had accomplished exactly what I had intended. I had caught Erin off guard and left her with an image of me, a reminder. My hope was that she would now start wondering about me, about us, and whatever *fun* she was having over the summer would be interrupted every so often with thoughts of me.

It turned out to be a long summer with no contact from Erin. I busied myself with work and my hometown friends and tried not to notice each day that passed without hearing from her. *Was she dating someone?* I pushed the creeping doubts out of my mind and even went on a few dates myself. Of course, the girls did not hold a candle to The Girl Who Wasn't Calling, but I was surprised to find dating other people was a nice distraction. An interesting metamorphosis was taking place within me. I felt stronger. I felt inexplicably more confident. I was disappointed for sure, but somehow it was empowering.

When the next semester started, I decided to stay in an off-campus apartment with some friends instead of staying in the dorms. I figured it would be easier on me if I put some space between us, especially if she were to start dating someone. I was right; being farther away from her, not seeing her as often made it easier for me to get through each day. When we did finally run into each other, I was careful not to appear jilted or bitter.

"Hey! Good to see you! How was your summer?" I was upbeat and all smiles. She seemed a bit caught off guard, as if she was expecting me to be angry at her for ignoring me all summer. Well, of course I was, but I knew better than to show it. This became my tactic—upbeat and unaffected.

Although I chose to live off campus to distance myself from Erin, it seemed to have the opposite effect. Much to my surprise, she started to call and stop by regularly. I didn't question the change. I just enjoyed the attention. Over the course of the semester, spending time with Erin became second nature. She made me laugh. She was audacious and sassy and made me laugh harder than anyone. We became close friends over those months. Erin started to open to me, and our conversations took on more depth. She teased me less, and I grew more comfortable with the way our relationship was evolving. My protective walls began to soften, and I began to let her in. As we grew closer, our physical desire for each other grew as well, and before long, Erin was spending every night with me at my apartment, although she still maintained we were not a couple. Even with that, I was happier than I ever thought possible.

The first semester of our sophomore year ended, and we were all preparing for the Christmas break. I called Erin so we could arrange to say goodbye in person before we parted ways for the next month. Her roommate answered the phone.

"Hi, Megan, it's John. Is Erin around?"

"Oh, no. Erin left two hours ago." I was silent as I let the words sink in.

Erin left two hours ago.

"You've got to be kidding me! She didn't even say goodbye?"

"Nope! She's gone!" The air deflated from my lungs.

"Okay, thanks, Megan. Have a nice Christmas." I hung up.

Erin left two hours ago. Son of a bitch. She did it again. She left without saying goodbye again.

My ears grew hot. I was fuming. We had grown so close over these past couple of months. How could she just leave me like that again? How much longer was I going to put up with this behavior? *Not much longer.*

I returned home to celebrate the holidays with my family as an angry young man. I was done with this roller-coaster ride. *Done.*

One day, my younger sister Laura came to me holding the mail.

"John, there's a card here for you." I felt as puzzled as she looked. I frowned a bit as I took the red envelope from her. Erin's return address was on the front. I blinked. *Really?* Feeling both annoyed and curious, I opened the envelope.

"Thinking of you," read the gold-embossed script on the front of the festive, green holiday card. I rolled my eyes. I opened it. "Wishing you all the joy of the holiday season." And there below in Erin's pretty, feminine handwriting were the words, "Love, Erin."

Love Erin? I rolled my eyes and laughed cynically. With a flick of the wrist, I tossed the card across the room. Laura stood staring at me, her brown eyes wide. I walked out of the room, leaving the card on the floor.

I did not respond to the card and instead spent the rest of my Christmas break with family and friends. When Erin would intrude on my thoughts, I would push her out of my mind.

Not now, Erin.

I returned to school with a fresh new outlook. I upgraded to a bigger apartment with more roommates, and I was now focusing on myself and improving my life. With Erin having consumed my energy, time, and my limited ability to focus during the first semester, my grades had suffered immensely.

No more.

Erin began calling as soon as she heard I had returned. Sometimes I would tell my roommates to tell her I wasn't home. Other times they would just tell her I was busy. Her calls became more frequent as she realized I was pulling away. I wasn't swayed. I had really had enough of the mind games and was relieved to finally focus on myself for a change.

After about three weeks, a letter arrived at the apartment addressed to me in familiar feminine handwriting. Curious, I took the letter to my room where I could open it in private. I sat on my bed and ripped open the envelope. Inside were two pages of petal-pink stationary with her neat, pretty handwriting filling both sides of each page.

That's quite a letter, I thought.

"Dear John," it began, the irony of that salutation was not lost on me, "my feelings have changed." Those four words began the most important letter I would ever read.

> I know you're probably upset with me, and I don't blame you. I want you to know that I have been doing a lot of thinking over these past few months. Over the past year, really. First, I want to apologize for the way I have treated you. I want you to understand that it has nothing to do with you and everything to do with me. I'm afraid. My feelings for you have grown a lot, and that scares me. I was not ready to find love again. I wanted time to be on my own and figure out what I wanted in my life, but then I met you, and that all changed. I knew right away that all I wanted was you, and I could not admit that to myself. It was not in my plan. So I ran. I pushed you away, and I was mean to you. I'm so sorry. You have always been so good to me, so patient. You let me be myself, as crazy as that can be sometimes, and you are probably the only person who really understands me. I honestly don't know how to act when you are around because I know you are really seeing me, and you accept me. I am afraid of how deeply I care about you because I know how badly it would hurt if I were to lose you. That's why I always left without saying goodbye. I knew it would hurt to say goodbye to you because I was going to miss you so much, so I just ran away. I'm afraid that I may have pushed you too far this time. I wanted you to know how I feel. I won't call or bother you. I'll let you think it over and make your decision. I hope you decide to give me another chance even though I may not deserve it. I'd love to introduce you to the other

side of me. I'd love the chance to love you the way you deserve to be loved.

Love,
Erin

I sat for a moment, stunned. I reread her words several more times, unable to believe she had actually written them to me. The letter was everything I had hoped for and everything I suspected. The truth was, she *had* crossed the line this last time when she left; she *had* pushed too far, and I was ready to let go of her. The fact that she knew that and owned up to all of it was all I needed for my walls to come crashing down. She'd made herself incredibly vulnerable to me.

I'd love the chance to love you the way you deserve to be loved. My heart skipped a bit when I read those words. Of course, I would give her another chance. I called her the next day and let her know I received her letter.

"You did?" She sounded uncharacteristically nervous.

"Yes, I did. Thank you. It meant a lot." She was silent. "I always hoped you would feel that way someday. I'm happy you do."

"Let's get together and talk, okay?" And with that, we started our twenty-four-year love story.

Six years later, I stood at the altar nervously awaiting the moment I would see my beautiful bride. I looked out among our family and friends who had gathered to share our day. The organ music announced the bride, and with a loud rustle, everyone stood and turned to face the back of the church. I craned my neck to see her.

When Erin appeared, there was an audible gasp throughout the church, and my breath was taken away. She stood there with sunlight streaming through a window behind her, adding to the radiant glow already emanating from her beautiful face. Her eyes met me through the white lace veil, and her smile mirrored mine. I had never seen anything so beautiful in all my life.

She walked slowly and purposefully down the aisle toward me on the arm of her father, just as she had always dreamed of doing. My beautiful girl was walking toward me to be my wife. When they reached me at the altar, her father lifted her veil, kissed her cheek, and taking her hand, transferred it to me. I held her hand tightly and stared into those sparkling, blue eyes. I felt my nervousness dissipate as we gazed at each other, and a sense of calm took over. This was just as it should be. This moment was perfect.

I spoke to her the sacred vows of marriage, "I agree to have and to hold you from this day forward, to honor and to cherish, for richer or poorer, for better or worse, in sickness and in health, till death do us part."

And Erin spoke them to me, looking deeply into my eyes with an expression of love that warmed my heart. There before God, friends, and family through the sanctity of marriage vows and ceremony, we offered ourselves to each other in every way with powerful obligations that we couldn't yet comprehend. It was official in an instant, and when the priest pronounced us husband and wife, I gently cupped her face in my hands and kissed my girl with every ounce of love I had.

CHAPTER 8

LESSONS REDISCOVERED

THESE WERE THE MOMENTS that allowed me to feel again through Him. Was that also His intention? To bring feeling back into my life? These were the joyful moments and feelings I knew I needed to gather up and hold on to.

For a fleeting moment, I wondered if allowing myself to feel this joy again would prolong my suffering but concluded He would not lead me to do this if that were true. I've committed to feel through Him; it was my calling. I felt grounded in that knowledge now. I could feel Him.

When I was a little boy, I saw things for myself and often learned about life the hard way. At some point, I realized that others saw me too. Among all those people, I found one to love, and it was Erin. We liked what we saw in each other, and we accepted that which wasn't so appealing. I cherished her for loving me. She saw something in me I could not. She saw me through God's eyes.

So many others liked Erin because they all liked what they saw too. Everyone was happiest around her.

I just need her to know I loved her and that I always will. She was so good for me.

Suddenly, Erin had simply vanished without warning, and we were all left stranded behind with only memories. I savored these most precious moments in time, but I cried over them as well. A brief flash took the one I loved, and now it illuminated these special moments.

I could use the light of my angel to help others whose bitterness is slowly killing them the way mine has been killing me.

Lighting the way for others might allow me to no longer revel in the ruins of the rubble but instead to pick up the gifts left behind, hold them tightly, and walk forward toward healing. Special memories of Erin would surely help illuminate the way.

Reviewing these mental snapshots all alone, I felt vulnerable and exposed. Something in the way He touched me compelled me to focus most of my attention on my favorite images. I immersed myself in each of these precious moments in time, desperately grasping for the feelings they evoked. I wanted to experience every sensation and emotion as thoroughly as I once had. I needed to relive them, and yet it was starting to break me.

As Erin once stood strong, I now yearned for that strength. It occurred to me that there were now two instances where a simple touch changed the course of my life and reshaped who I was. The first occurred when I physically reached out and touched Erin for the first time all those years ago to confirm she was real, and the second was when I was spiritually touched by Him.

I must rely on His strength now.

Searching for answers I didn't know the questions to, I shifted from a mental visit to my past to a more physical one. I had stumbled upon an old box of childhood relics, and as I sifted through, I discovered a stack of early report cards that clearly told my story.

"John does not work well with others."

"John does not use his time wisely or work well independently."

"John does not demonstrate self-control."

Geez. Did John do anything well?

Having since been diagnosed with ADHD, the symptoms now shouted out at me from the yellowed pages. The feedback from my earliest teachers clearly described a child who was struggling with faulty wiring. It was also clear that effective treatments for this condition had developed quite a bit *after* my days in elementary school.

At the time, I was oblivious to these issues my teachers were describing. Inherently I had known I was different from the other children in my class but didn't have the capacity to understand why. As an adult looking back on the child I had once been, I realized as I read these comments how unaware I had been that there were others right next to me and that they had feelings too. What troubled me became very clear in these moments. I could now see how I had adapted over the years to compensate for my impairment and how that had impacted my view of the world, my ability to cope, and consequently, the man I had grown into.

A flood of fragmented memories from school and my childhood home began to spin through my mind like a vortex. Nothing made sense, but somehow it all made sense.

Now that I had begun this trek forward, I was driven to learn more about the events in my early life that became the foundation for who I was to become. I needed something that would help me to find my way.

At the bottom of the box, I found my very first report card. It was from Mrs. Mundy's kindergarten class. This was the very class where I pushed that boy down after he took my block. It was incredible to be holding it in my hand, this accounting of my teacher who had witnessed firsthand those events that had become such powerful memories for me.

What insight could she offer me after all these years? How might this help me to heal?

I anxiously began reading the reports from Mrs. Mundy. As expected, they detailed my difficulties exhibiting self-control. I was touched by the fact that she knew me so well, and her comments were surprisingly caring and insightful.

> John is very capable, but he is so very wound up that he is not using his ability to his advantage. He functions best when he has twice as much to do as the other children, but this is not always possible. John is making satisfactory progress, but he still is very, very active. There has been an

improvement in John's self-control. He is trying. He does very well in number and readiness activities. He expresses himself well. John is a delightful little boy, so ready to smile and eager to be helpful. He has made very satisfactory progress this year. He has the ability to be an excellent student. Best of luck to John and his family in the new school and home. Will miss you.

As I read, my eyes filled with tears. Through my teacher's compassionate words, I saw myself as a young boy who was trying to work through his issues with varying degrees of success.

John is a delightful little boy, so ready to smile and eager to be helpful.

There has been an improvement in John's self-control. He is trying.

These words ushered in the staggering realization that I had been seeing myself through a distorted lens for most of my life. I had always assumed my teacher knew me as a bad child, a flawed boy who challenged her and made her life a living hell each day. I lived with this shameful, distorted image. It became the foundation for who I believed myself to be.

As I read Mrs. Mundy's words written nearly forty years prior, I looked at myself for the first time with compassion. Instead of a problem child, I saw a kind, well-intentioned little boy who was struggling with a real impairment beyond his control and who was *trying his best.*

These are more of the positive feelings that I need to hold onto.

I knew I needed to heal myself to rebuild my crumbled foundation. I now realized that in order to accomplish this, I needed to let go of the warped beliefs I held about myself and replace them with more accurate information.

I have to go back there.

This sudden urge to go back to my elementary school two states away to visit Mrs. Mundy's classroom was overwhelming and totally out of character for me. My logical mind told me it made no sense. Something else or Someone else was saying something very different.

CHAPTER 9

THE WALLS CAME DOWN

Now a middle-aged man who may not have much time left, there was a constant drip of fear this would all end badly. In spite of recent revelations, my go-to instincts of fear, anger, and shame continued to challenge me as each one battled for dominance.

My new outlook had made me even more aware of these divergent forces, but I was not yet able to master them.

I selfishly questioned who I hurt more for, myself or my own children? Inside my testimony, the truth must emerge. I hoped embarking on this journey and sifting through years of distorted thinking would make me able to feel right again.

"God, please help me because this is all killing me."

I was experiencing an emotional pain unlike any I had felt before. Enduring it proved to be a formidable test, and of course, it was one I was not prepared for. It felt as if I was being hit from every side, and with each blow, I grew more uncertain I would emerge the victor, something I could not allow.

Before becoming ill, I had naturally clung to life above all else. With the new possibility of my own death occurring sooner than I had ever imagined for myself, my mission had now become to die in everlasting peace.

Visions of Erin's face, pale with death, the strained, grief-stricken faces of my children, and my own face, drawn and sunken with illness and emotional exhaustion pulled me away from the good thoughts I so desperately needed and plunged me headlong into a dark abyss.

Am I a poster child for misery?

As usual, I was experiencing too many feelings at once. I was overloaded.

What happened to that glorious feeling that had made sense of it all?

I forced myself to turn my focus away from the dark images that haunted me and were threatening to pull me under. I desperately groped and searched for even a trace of that calm, knowing feeling I had experienced when He touched me. In that incredible moment, there had been an undeniable feeling of reunion. It was as if he had been making Himself known to me once more.

Where are you now? I'm sinking.

I pleaded for Him to return. I had been commissioned to play this part, and I accepted. I had agreed to revisit the events in my life that had damaged me and, in doing so, to learn my lessons and allow goodness to emerge from the pain. I had agreed to open myself up to scrutiny, to lay myself bare as I did so in hopes of building my character, and God willing, to figure all this out.

We all have to answer to someone.

The urge to return to my kindergarten classroom continued to grow, and before long, I found myself en route to Cook School in Plainfield, New Jersey, preparing to face one of the most compelling moments of my childhood—the day I pushed that boy.

As I drove, the moment replayed in my mind as it had countless times since it happened.

Why is this moment such a life changer for me?

This childhood moment had become the hardest one to shake off. It haunted me, challenged me; it stared me down.

Why?

I then considered the moment from a more neutral perspective. I had been so young at the time, only on this earth for five years. That boy had taken my block, and no one had ever taken anything from me before. My reaction was primal.

What haunts me most about this moment?

The expression of fear on the face of that little boy was what haunted me, quickly followed by the shame in knowing I caused it simply because I could not control my emotions.

As I drove, my thoughts continued to flow, and with them, new realizations began to emerge. The manner in which I handled my anger had never seemed normal. My anger was almost always disproportionate to the situation. It then dawned on me that I might be transmuting other emotions through my anger. I realized that my shame, fear, and regret were all automatically converted to anger, directed inward yet outwardly acted upon.

As I pulled into the parking lot of the school, the red brick building was at once familiar to me. Clutching my report card, I walked up to the main entrance, pulled open the heavy white door, and took my first step back in time.

I recognized the smell first—only to be described as quintessentially elementary school—an odd combination of books, janitorial cleaning products, crayons, and school lunch. The front lobby was exactly as I had remembered; the only thing that seemed different was that it had been much larger in my mind's eye.

That's because I was only five years old the last time I stood here.

That same powerful force that brought me back here now propelled me down the hallway to the administrative office. It had been forty years since I walked these halls, and as I did, the very memories I was so desperately seeking began calling out to me with every step I took. It was relatively quiet, as I noted. One little boy walked past me, presumably on his way to class, gripping a laminated hall pass.

I entered the office where a middle-aged woman sat behind the front desk. She looked up at me and smiled pleasantly.

"May I help you?" she asked.

"I'm not sure, but I hope so," I began. I wasn't totally clear on why I was there myself, only that I needed to be. "I attended this school about forty years ago for one year, my kindergarten year. I was wondering if it would be possible to see the classroom I had been in."
She blinked, surprised, and her face lit up.

"Oh, that's amazing! Really?"

"Yes, in fact, I even still have my report card." I pulled it from the small manila envelope and held it out for her. Intrigued, she took the folded, pale-blue card stock and carefully opened it. As her eyes scanned the handwritten report card, she smiled warmly. Handing it back, she commented, "It is so nice that you still have that! What a wonderful memento!"

With that, another woman, presumably the principal, stepped out of the small adjoining office and looked curiously at me.

"This is John Whitmeyer, a former student. He has come back to visit us today! He even still has his report card!" The principal looked pleasantly surprised and invited me into her office. As I sat down, I glanced at the diplomas on the wall and took note of her neat desk.

"So you were a student here?" she said, taking her seat.

"Yes, believe it or not, I attended kindergarten here about forty years ago. Mrs. Mundy was my teacher."

"I'm sorry to say I didn't know her."

"Well, it has been quite a while. I would be very surprised if she were still here." I smiled. "It's kind of an odd request, but I was wondering if it would be possible to see my old classroom."

"Sure, I'd be happy to take you!" The principal smiled broadly and stood up. As we walked out of the office, I heard the bell ring, and within seconds, the hallway was filled and bustling with students.

As I followed the principal, I remembered the classroom was just a short distance around the corner. I was correct. When we arrived, I stood before the familiar large oak-trimmed door and looked through the window. The classroom was filled with kindergartners, just as it had been when I was last there. My eyes swept the room. It looked exactly as I had remembered.

"My gosh," I murmured, "it hasn't changed at all!" I remembered those tilt-in glass windows that lined the outside wall and the big radiators below them.

"This school has many of the original features. It was very well built and has really stood the test of time. It looks the same as you remembered?" I nodded, lost for words. I glanced down at the gleaming silver doorknob and realized it might even be the same one I'd last grasped with my child-sized hand. I took in the vibrant classroom decor, all the things you might expect to see; children's artwork and large ABCs in primary colors adorned the walls. I watched as the children settled in their seats while listening attentively to their teacher. They were so little, so young—babies really.

Just like I was, all those years ago.

My world was now spinning fast. I was longing for answers, and I prayed that this inviting door that had long since closed behind me would serve a new purpose, a gateway to unlocking the past. I hoped to uncover something here. I needed something from this old classroom, this very place where my self-admonishment began.

After forty years, I had still failed to erase the haunting scene from my mind. That little boy's face with frightened eyes still stared into mine, serving as an eerie reminder of my many wrongdoings. I didn't know his name, but I could tell he was shocked that day, and I wondered if his mind was as seared with this experience as mine was.

It all happened so quickly; he was not prepared for it. I had knocked him down and left him there to struggle, alone in the rubble. Those blocks I used had seemed sturdy and strong, yet in an instant, they all came tumbling down. I had inflicted suffering on someone.

Now as I peered into the very place where my troubles seemed to originate, I realized my sense of shame I carried with me had long since been superseded with a feeling of compassion for the boy I pushed over. I began to understand that as a child I had been oblivious to the impact of my actions on the others around me and that as an adult I had been unable to forgive myself for that. I had been holding my five-year-old self to an adult standard.

As I looked at these little children fidgeting in their seats, trying to remain focused on their lessons, I saw myself in them. Now that I was an adult, it was time to start focusing more on empathy and compassion for others and for myself.

I left the school with a new sense of calm that told me I had accomplished what was intended. I had learned a valuable lesson that would aid in my healing and in my journey toward inner peace.

Just a short distance away, I turned right on Coolidge Street, stopping in front of the house where I was born. A collage of fragmented memories flashed before my eyes and challenged me to remember, to piece together my childhood. Eagerly I looked up and down the familiar street, soaking in every moment.

I could remember what my house looked like inside and out. The tiny round pool in the backyard and that aged timber tactfully nailed to the walls of that tired, old shed were etched in perfect detail in my mind. Everything came rushing back. My roots were here. It all started here.

I walked across the front lawn, as I had so many times in the past. Cautiously approaching the brick steps in front, I remembered tripping on them while waiting for my preschool car pool. I could see myself there lying flat out and screaming, blood dripping from my forehead. My mother could only wave the car pool on.

I knocked on the front door, but no one answered. I was hoping to talk to someone who lived there and perhaps be able to take a quick peek inside. In my mind's eye, I could clearly see my large bedroom awash in the gleaming sunlight from my window and those uneven basement stairs where I tripped and dropped that can of juice, almost shearing off a finger. These memories, stored for decades, stirred deep feelings within me, and I began to feel anxious.

Why are my memories of this time so negative?

A deep-seated fear threatened to run rampant inside me, and I realized I felt deserving of my ill fate. Refusing to give in to it, I consciously pushed off the darkness that was attempting to dim the light I had just discovered within myself at that school.

I recognized it and decided I would instead attest to goodness that shines along a dark road. I once again committed myself to follow this guidance and fight back uncertainty the whole way.

As I readied myself to leave, I circled my car and stood for a moment, looking back down Coolidge Street for what may be the last time. I saw myself as a little boy walking home from school. I looked at that little boy closely, staring right into his blue eyes, *my* blue eyes, and he stared back into mine. In that moment of clarity, I recognized myself as the product of his perceptions.

As I drove home, thoughts scattered throughout my mind like a tricky puzzle strewn about on the floor. As a test of will, now more than ever, I was determined to crouch down and gather up every intricate piece. I had to ensure that my life would be made whole once again before my time ran out.

There was a balance to be found between looking carefully at negative events of the past to learn from them and dwelling endlessly in darkness with no growth. That kindergarten mistake and every difficult lesson that followed had helped to mold me, and I now needed to learn more about who I had become. I was ready to take a good look at my shortcomings, not with the intention of berating myself but with a new sense of compassion and desire to heal.

I returned home with a new feeling of mercy for that frightened boy in my class and for myself. This new sense of compassion helped me to identify within myself the emotions most in need of healing—fear, pain, carelessness, isolation, and resentment. Erin had helped me manage these emotions, and without her, they had taken the upper hand. It was time for me to take back control and step forward into healing.

CHAPTER 10

LOST WORDS

MONTHS HAD PASSED SINCE Erin's death, but the outpouring of support from friends and family continued. My days were spent opening thoughtful cards from the many different people who knew Erin and loved her.

Beginning immediately, friends organized a rotation and brought meals for myself and the kids three days each week. Another group of her friends arranged for and paid our housekeeper Martha to visit twice each month, and someone even planted new colorful flowers in our planters each new season. This kind of thoughtful support was beyond anything I could have ever expected and was a testament to the kind of person Erin was. We lived in a magical place, this small town of Trumbull, the place of Erin's birth.

I found my way to a website where one can light a candle in honor of someone who had passed. It was amazing to read back through these comments and see so clearly the effect Erin had on so many lives. The fact that she passed away in the prime of her life compounded my pain. She wasn't done living. She had so much more to do.

This clearly hit home with many others as well, and their sympathetic expressions touched me deeply and brought comfort.

Perhaps it was Erin's friend Janet who summarized it best, "The world was definitely a warmer, happier place with Erin in it. She lit up our lives with her smile, her crazy sense of humor, her overwhelming love for life. She had such a special heart, and she made room in it for everyone she knew and loved."

Sentiments like this inspired hope in me, and witnessing the outpouring of kindness brought comfort. My own internal conflicts had me torn and confused, but every kind heart that surrounded us was building something special in me.

As a way to start organizing my thoughts, I began jotting them down along with the onslaught of memories that were now flooding my mind. Writing *anything* was highly unusual for me, and I wasn't sure why this had become my go-to coping mechanism. I had never taken a liking to reading. In fact, I couldn't think of a book I had started and actually finished because my overactive mind was distracted away from the words just sitting idle on the page. Writing had been even more of a challenge for me, so the idea that it would have ever become a way for me to cope with emotional trauma was quite unexpected.

Interestingly, the more I wrote, the more comfort I took from it, and soon I was spending most of my free time articulating my thoughts and feelings. Memories, especially those from my early childhood, became a primary focus. The way I felt as a child was strikingly similar to the way I was feeling now.

As I continued to wage my emotional battles, I was still engaged in my physical one. My illness had not disappeared with Erin. It continued to make the simplest of daily tasks a challenge.

I arrived at the medical center for one of my frequent intravenous treatments and sat alone, a needle in my arm, anxiously watching the drip of my medication. Looking around me, I saw other patients, all hoping the same drip could save them too. Drip, drip, drip. So many people with so many problems—I was not the only one struggling.

When I arrived home, I sat down, as I did every day, to pencil some thoughts into my journal. This routine had now become an integral part of my healing process. The notebook now contained the most intimate and meaningful words I had ever written, words that acted as a salve to my gaping wounds. As I looked around for my spiral-bound lifeline, the high-pitched ringing of panic began to set in.

Where could it be?

With a sinking feeling in the pit of my stomach, I remembered I had taken it with me to my treatment at the medical center, almost an hour away.

Oh my god, I placed it on the counter in the cafeteria after buying the water and two hard-boiled eggs. It's gone.

I could feel the familiar flush of an oncoming rage. I clenched my teeth, grabbed my hair tightly in both hands, and began angrily pacing, berating myself. Once again, because of my own stupid carelessness, something precious and irreplaceable was gone.

Furious and sliding back into old patterns as easily as a well-worn pair of slippers, I looked around for something to break. Uncontrolled rage overtook me. I grabbed a wooden kitchen chair and began slamming it violently against the floor. This was a pounding that I deserved.

How could I let this happen? My words. They were gone.

My adrenaline raged into an inferno, and I grabbed the seat of the chair with one hand and flipped it over effortlessly with seemingly almighty strength. This was quickly followed by another chair thrown, banging loudly to the floor. The third one was kicked across the room and, with a splintering crash, bounced off the wall.

So careless! What was I thinking leaving it there on the counter? How could I be so stupid?

With each passing moment, the rage inside me continued to boil over. I was sweating, short of breath, and occasionally, I smacked my own head in frustration. This was the way I learned, wasn't it? Next time maybe I would be more careful with things that were important to me. How I hated learning these lessons. Something that was extremely important to me had been lost because I didn't handle it with enough care.

Why do I always have to lose something to learn the lesson?

The words I'd written—toiled over—were gone forever. I was at my weakest, and that simple fact crushed me. My rant continued until my thirteen-year-old daughter, Brittany, stepped in as the unlikely voice of reason.

"Calm down, Dad. This is not necessary. You need to *calm right down*." She stood staring at me, disgusted by my maniacal display. Calming myself during one of my tirades was nearly impossible for me. Erin hated when I did this.

"Oh, don't be such a baby. You're acting foolish," she would say and thus would trigger the process of calming me down.

Startled, I looked at Brittany standing there, watching my childish behavior with disdain and saw myself through her eyes. This was not the example to be setting for my children. This was not the father they needed, and this was not an appropriate way to handle anger. I felt the rage dying down within me.

"I'm sorry, Britt," I said, catching my breath. "You're right." Satisfied that I was calming down, she helped me pick up the chairs and then strode from the room to resume her childhood.

I began to once again think rationally.

I should call the doctor's office and try to reach someone who could look for the journal for me.

I made a few quick phone calls and was finally connected to a gentleman who was on security detail for the evening.

"Sir, please, I hope you can help me. I've left something in the cafeteria. It's a five-subject, black notebook. I think I left it on the counter near the cash register. Please, can you check for me?"

"Sure, let me take a quick look." The open line echoed as he dropped the receiver on the counter. I heard his footsteps on the tile floor fade away. I was in knots at this point, frantically awaiting his return.

Well, this is a much more productive and civilized way to handle this situation.

I felt a familiar wave of shame as I thought of my out-of-control behavior. Within a few moments, I heard the security guard's footsteps approaching the desk, and he picked up the receiver. "Yup, I have it here. It was on the counter by the register, black cover, and it says 'Five Star' on the front." My jaw fell to the floor as a wave of immense relief washed over me. I felt strong again. He found my words.

"I'm forty-five minutes away, and I am leaving now. How late will you be there?"

"I'm working until ten. I'm not going anywhere until then." I thanked him repeatedly and told him he could expect me soon. Hanging up the phone, I looked up, surprised to see Brittany standing there. I hadn't heard her come back in.

"They found my journal. They have it! I'm going back to the medical center to pick it up."

Brittany smiled and shook her head. "See, all of that for nothing! That was ridiculous, Dad!" she scolded. I couldn't have agreed more.

"I know, honey. I'm sorry. I need to work on that. Thank you for reminding me." I gave her a quick hug and was out the door to recover my priceless words.

I stared straight ahead, speeding down the highway on a mission. I would not be able to relax until I had that journal in my hands again, but I already felt grateful. I couldn't believe the security guard had found it. I was never that fortunate.

I am so damn lucky. I said a quick "Thank You" to Him.

As usual, the radio was on as I drove, and I was only half-listening. After a song or two, I began to notice a distinct pattern in the lyrics. This was notable because anyone who knew me knew I never heard song lyrics. Melodies were all that caught my attention. The words to songs just tumbled by, their meaning lost on me.

On this particular evening, it seemed the lyrics to every song I heard were directly connected with what I was experiencing. With each song, I grew more astounded, and it became tough to stay focused on the road.

Is this some kind of message? It certainly felt that way. As I felt myself relax into the music, my mind drifted a bit. I revisited my recent tirade in the kitchen and shook my head.

My God, have I turned out just like her?

My mother's extreme mood swings—most likely brought on by mental illness of one sort or another—had peppered my childhood with similar displays of rage. My sisters and I never knew what might set off one of her destructive tantrums, so we learned to tiptoe through life, fearful of stirring the demons within her.

As an adult, I made a conscious effort to approach my life much differently than my mother had in fear of turning out like her. This outburst of mine witnessed by my daughter was a bit too similar, and I recognized it.

No more.

I knew I was driving too fast, but I was extremely anxious to hold my found words. I decided whatever cash I had in my pocket would go to the security guard who found my journal. I had no idea how much was there, but I had decided I would give him all of it.

Pulling into the parking lot of the medical building, I came to a screeching halt. My truck rocked back and forth from the sudden stop as I frantically removed the keys from the ignition. Trying not to appear too desperate, I entered the building and saw a gentleman standing at the desk.

"Hi, my name is John. I called about the black notebook."

"Yes, I have it right here." The security guard smiled and reached down for something on the desk in front of him. I immediately recognized my journal, and relief flooded over me.

"I am so grateful to you for finding this for me. I decided as I drove down here that I would give you every dollar in my pocket, however much that is." He blinked, surprised.

Reaching into my pocket, I pulled out a tight wad of money. There were several twenty-dollar bills, a five-dollar bill, and some singles totaling $108.00. When I was done counting, I slid it over to him and said, "Well, it's not much, but I insist you take it because the words in this notebook are priceless to me." He handed me the notebook, and speechless, he reached down and picked up the money off the desk. When he looked back up at me, his eyes were filled with tears. Composing himself, he laughed. "What do you have written in there? The cure for cancer or something?" I laughed because to me it was the cure for so much more.

CHAPTER 11

◆

PRICELESS GIFTS

THERE IS NO TIMETABLE for grief. Isn't that what they say? One morning, I found myself in Erin's large walk-in closet, staring at the dozens and dozens of empty shoes that lined the shelves. I marveled at the fact that she was able to so effectively walk in every one of them. Each pair from her tennis shoes to her Jimmy Choos, varying in color and style, represented a multidimensional human being. Everything she had done as a wife and mother, sister, daughter, colleague, and wonderful friend had happened in these shoes that she had chosen to wear on those journeys. There would be no more journeys. She was gone, and the reality of it was as shocking and gut-wrenching as it was the first time it hit me.

Erin, where are you?

This warm, vibrant soul had suddenly vanished without warning, and perhaps most tragically, she never got to say goodbye.

But where did you go?

Forever removed from us were things that had become an assumed part of our every day. I couldn't imagine that we would never again experience the sweet tone of her voice or the soft caress of her hand reassuring us that she loved us. The abandoned shoes before me represented my new stark reality—empty. My friend, my wife, my love—that nurturing soul was gone, and it was too surreal to believe.

Erin had been bestowed a life, and I was forever grateful to have shared part of it with her. Together we had created life, three times over, blessings beyond comprehension. I felt the swell of honor as I thought about caring for our children—her legacy.

I will raise our children as you would have wanted, but to do this, I must find my way.

There might be no timetable for grief, but there was no time clock for parenting either, and I knew I had to get it together to be the parent I needed to be for our children.

Brittany appeared before me one evening, disheveled in pajamas. "Dad, will you tuck me in?" She was my oldest and my most independent. I knew she must have needed some extra comforting and support, so I took the opportunity to lie down with her and talk.

"How are you doing, Britt?" I asked quietly. She paused for a moment before answering.

"I'm okay. I just miss Mommy."

"I know, doll. I know. I miss her too." I choked up as I held her close to me, hoping she felt my love, hoping it was enough.

God, Erin, how do I do this without you?

I closed my eyes and listened as Brittany's steady, wakeful breathing grew deeper and knew she had drifted off to sleep.

My sweet girl. I continued to hold her, wanting her to feel safe and secure while she slept. Her small bed was comfortable and warm, and I felt myself getting drowsy.

Suddenly, the warmth of Erin's glow shone down on me. Her presence was brilliant and a sight to behold. I reached my arms high to hold her, extending my arms under hers and curving them up until my hands held the back of each of her shoulders. I rested my cheek on her chest, felt the warmth of her arms holding me to her, and did not utter one word. No words were needed; there was simply calm knowing.

This magnificent being, so tall and powerful, just held me. The energy between us was unmistakable. It was Erin, only *more*. I knew it was Erin, but it was Erin in her purest, most vibrant, radiant form, unencumbered by earthly limitations. This was *Erin*. The entire being I sensed within the person I knew and loved.

I awoke sobbing, overwhelmed with emotion, yet there was a sense of peace I hadn't felt in a very long time.

Could she feel that through me?

This enchanted dream was the first time since her death that our paths had crossed. I had called on her for help with Brittany, and she came to me.

Of course, she did.

She had been even more beautiful than I remembered, and I could feel the warmth of her compassion and reassurance. I knew that she was telling me she was happy with my growth and that I was caring for her children and doing it well. My heart was elated. I had received the confirmation I had been desperately yearning for: *I was not alone.*

In the coming days, I continued to ponder my dream.

Was that even a dream? It was unlike any I'd ever had before.

I relived it over and over in my mind. I had never felt such a powerful sense of unconditional love; it was given and received simultaneously in pure silence. Words had not been necessary. The flow of energy and emotion between us was effortless and natural and left me with a sense of serenity. It was reminiscent of the feeling I had experienced when He touched me. *This was Him.*

Written words had been an important part of my life with Erin. Her words carefully penned in her letter to me over Christmas break decades earlier had conveyed her thoughts and feelings to me from miles away. The moment I felt the energy of love behind her written words, my life was changed forever. *Our* lives were changed forever.

We often searched for the right cards that expressed things we felt at any given moment. Erin always seemed to find the perfect card to capture and reflect whatever chapter we were in; they were like a written record of our relationship together.

"Dad! Where are the batteries? The remote won't work!" I looked up to see Johnny standing in the living room, holding up the useless TV remote. I pulled myself slowly to my feet, wincing with the pain that had become part of my daily existence.

I opened The Drawer. Every house has one, the drawer that collects odds and ends that have no other place to go. Our house had several of those drawers because I had three kids and didn't have the energy to make sure household items made it back to their rightful places. I opened one such drawer and rummaged through the menagerie of pens, magnets, tape, and take-out menus in hopes of finding some batteries. Nothing.

"Sorry, fella, maybe in here." I tugged open another drawer. As I dug around in it, I felt an odd stack of papers and pulled them out; some slipped onto the floor. It was a stack of greeting cards. Johnny instinctively bent down and scooped up the cards for me. My thoughtful little guy knew it was hard for me to bend down.

"What are these for, Dad?" He looked the cards over as he handed them to me.

"These," I replied, sifting through them, "are cards your mom and I gave to each other over the years. Wow, I can't believe she saved all of these." It was so Erin. She was a saver. I smiled as I felt the now-familiar lump forming in my throat again.

"Can I see them?" he asked softly. In that moment, I saw in his eyes the need to connect with his mother. He needed to feel her, even if just through her sentiments written to me in a birthday card from five years earlier. I handed them to him, and he sat down on the couch. He began pouring over them slowly.

"Whatcha doin'?" Kylie sprang into the room, practicing her cheerleading moves while looking over Johnny's shoulder. "What are those?" I saw her recognize her mother's writing, and she became still. "Are those from Mom?" Her blonde brows furrowed a bit.

"Yes. And I'm looking at them, Kylie." Johnny turned slightly away from his older sister, anticipating older-sister shenanigans.

"Dad, where are our baby books?" Kylie turned to me. "Didn't Mom make us each our own baby book?"

She was right, and her timing could not have been better.

"Yes, she did," I replied smiling. Johnny looked up from the cards, blue eyes wide with curiosity. "And she worked very hard on them for each of you. I know just where they are."

When I returned to the family room, I could see that word had traveled quickly. All three of my children were now sitting on the couch, waiting for me to return with their baby books. The sight was at once adorable and heartbreaking.

I handed each child their thick binder, crafted with love by the person we all missed so badly our hearts ached.

Kylie eagerly opened hers, anxious to reconnect with her mother. On every page of each child's book, Erin had painstakingly cut out photos and mementos and wrote little notes to each child about things they loved, things she loved about them, funny moments, and important milestones.

In Kylie's book, among the countless priceless photos was one that was especially powerful. Erin stood smiling down at a five-year-old Kylie, shielding them both from the rain with a polka-dot umbrella. Kylie's smiling face, beaming up at her mother with pure adoration, summed up their relationship perfectly. A little note was posted next to it, written in Erin's pretty, feminine script.

"Kylie's last week of kindergarten. It doesn't seem possible! How we are going to miss our long mornings together! Your sleeping until nine and our shopping trips and lunch! It's off to a full day of first grade! How we will miss each other! I love you!"

Kylie took this all in thoughtfully.

"I remember this. I remember going shopping with Mommy every day!"

Brittany carefully turned each colorful page in her book.

"I was the smallest in my class?" she asked, reading Erin's note to her.

"Only two and a half years old when you started nursery school! You were the smallest and the youngest. You tried so hard and always made us proud. You loved school from day one!"

"Yes, that's right!" I replied, looking over her shoulder at the photo of a tiny Britt with straight, shiny bangs reaching into the sand table in her nursery-school classroom. "You were always a little bit of a thing! You still are!"

Johnny had been quietly looking through his blue binder in his own little world while the girls exclaimed and showed each other photos from their books.

The cover of Johnny's book read, "Mommy's Prince Charming," with a photo of Erin and a three-year-old blonde Johnny, their faces pressed close together with matching blue eyes and smiles.

"You were her little pot of gold, Johnny. Her boy. She was so proud of her son." I smiled at him. He studied the photos of toddler Johnny eating a red Popsicle, cheeks and lips sticky and red. He laughed and read aloud from his book.

"The summer of 2003, your favorite treat was a *pop*! I would say the word, and you would kick up your feet and run to the freezer and say, 'Mmmu, mmmu!' How you love your pops! And we love you to have them."

We sat and cherished each photo and note from Erin to her children. They were priceless gifts. With her written words and carefully selected images, she was able to convey to each child who they were to her, how much she loved them, and the wonder and magic each of them had brought to her life. They were able to feel the energy behind her words and receive the message of unconditional motherly love she had for each of them.

"Listen to this!" Brittany exclaimed, holding up her book so she could read aloud from it. "My beautiful Brittany, I cannot even begin to explain the fear and anticipation that filled me up inside before you were born."

"Is that true, Dad? You and Mommy were scared?"

"*Of course*, we were!" I laughed. "We were really excited, of course, but really nervous because you were our first baby! Your mom and I wanted to make sure we did everything right." All three faces looked surprised. "We even went to the hospital too early, and they sent us home!"

"What was it like when you saw me?" she asked shyly.

"Oh, it was love at first sight. We both looked at you, and our worlds changed forever. Neither of us had ever loved anyone or anything as much as we loved you." Britt smiled softly and looked back at her book.

"I had black hair?" she asked, laughing. "Why? Where did that come from?"

"Oh my gosh, you had a head full of crazy thick, black hair. It stuck up all over. It was adorable! Your mom would put bows and headbands in it every day. Every day you were in a new little outfit, decked out from head to toe. You were her baby doll. Her dolly."

"I thought Mommy dressed *me* up every day!" Kylie exclaimed.

"Oh, she did! She dressed *all* of you to the nines!" I laughed. "Kylie, you were so tiny. It was astonishing! Only six pounds, you were the tiniest little baby we had ever seen!" She smiled. "So precious. You had the tiniest little fingers and toes and no hair whatsoever." We all laughed. "Mommy loved you so much before she even met you. She talked to you every night before you were born."

"What about me?" Johnny chimed in.

"Oh," I began, "Johnny, you were Mommy's *boy*, her little prince. When you were born, she didn't want to hand you over to anyone. She just held you and stared at your chubby little face and smiled. She said when she handed you over to me, it was like she was handing me a miracle. Our family was complete when you were born, John."

Everyone grew quiet, looking intently at their pages filled and overflowing with love from their mother. "Your mom loved each one of you unconditionally and individually. You each have different qualities that are special about you, and your mom recognized all of them. I'm so happy she wrote it all down for you so you never forget just how much she saw in you and how she adored you."

I talked to my children about what they remembered, making sure they would never forget the simple things like hugs and kisses, the laughter, and the love they shared with their beloved mother.

Brittany spoke up again softly, "This is so nice. Listen to what she wrote."

"You have a gentle soul. Anyone should consider themselves lucky to be your friend. You are an amazing child not because you are the nicest, smartest, or the most athletic, though all do apply, but you are a kind and giving person. You have always made your dad and I proud." She looked up, and her beautiful eyes were bright with unshed tears.

"That's all true, Britt. You *are* all of those things. And we are so proud of the person you are. I know your mom is watching over you, she is watching over all of you." I swallowed hard, feeling my daughter's pain.

"She said I have beauty, wit, and passion for fashion!" Kylie laughed, holding up the page to show the note. "Brittany, she says we are different flowers from the same garden!"

"That you are, girls! That you are." I laughed. They were quite different in a lot of ways but were very close sisters. Erin had described them perfectly.

As the kids busied themselves with their books, I picked up the newly discovered cards and began to look through them. As I read each card, I began to notice she had written the letter "J" in John as a heart. I felt the familiar cold pang of heartache at this realization.

Had she always done that? I never noticed. I blinked back tears.

That would only mean something to us, and I could not believe I never noticed her sweet gesture to me at any point during our entire quarter century together. Every time Erin wrote my name, she drew a heart, the same piece of me I asked her to accept when she passed and the place in me where she would remain forever.

> John, after ten years together, never did I think we would be where we are. It has been a very busy and rewarding time. Our three little beauties and still I can say my heart beats for you, even more than it did ten years ago. I love you. I love you. Did I say it enough?

Reading her written words provided comfort in realizing that I had offered her all of me. I knew this because she told me right here in these cards over and over.

> It wouldn't have worked between us if it wasn't challenging. I wasn't like the other girls, I'll admit. I remember when I first saw you and spoke to you, and I let you touch me. What was I feeling?

The same things that you were feeling, of course.
I couldn't help falling in love with you because
you could hear what my heart was saying.

This was what kept me from giving up on her when we first met. I *could* hear what her heart was saying, long before she was ready to speak the words.

I have said so many things to you over the years,
and it boils down to the fact that only a few words
really matter. Instead, it's what you showed me.
You saw me every day and knew me like no other.
You saw my soul.

I still see it, Erin. I still feel it.

Things were so good for so long, then we were
struck with difficulty. That day after we saw
your doctor and we cried together, that was the
moment I knew I loved the right person. We can
weather any storm as long as we stick together.
John, you will always be my hero. You are an
amazing man for all that you have done for us,
and for that, I will spend forever just loving,
loving, loving you. If you are ever in doubt,
always know I loved you yesterday, today, and all
the days you have to come.

Just as I had wanted my children to read her words and feel her love, I was now doing the same. I, too, desperately needed to reconnect with her in this way to remember these moments she had catalogued for us. I needed to feel the energy of love behind her written words.

Erin and I were so far apart now. In fact, she was out of body and no longer part of my physical world. She went her own way, leaving our comfort zone. I begged of her in my mind and heart not to venture too far away because we needed her. How could we maintain an interpersonal relationship in the face of this untimely but natural separation?

To our children, Erin was love, safety, and comfort. Unlike my own mother, Erin was nurturing, as a mother should be, a maternal soul, an astute educator who earned these accolades. I was determined to nourish, protect, love, and cultivate our children the way that Erin did.

Chapter 12

Reconciliation

I HAD TO FIND peace and acceptance, or my unrest would haunt me for eternity. I couldn't allow that for my children and those who loved me. Reconciliation must be found, or my remaining years would pass miserably.

Therefore, I prepared for my first Christmas without Erin. I found myself walking about wherever I was, feeling drained. St. Patrick's Day, Mother's Day, Halloween, (which was also her birthday), then Thanksgiving. It was our first round of holidays without her, and soon a new year would begin, a year that Erin had not lived to see.

On New Year's Eve, I'd always tipped a full glass to Erin, but now my glass was empty and dry. I didn't want to spoil everyone's fun. Christmas was supposed to be a happy time. It was the season to be thankful for the love we shared and good health we enjoyed. I wrestled with feelings of jealousy, being deprived of things that enriched others. I felt scorned and heartbroken, wondering why she had to go.

Every single thing was different. Traditions that had once been festive and fun now reminded me that people and the rest of the world were moving on without Erin. Seeing people laughing and smiling felt like a betrayal.

How can they possibly be having fun right now? Erin is gone.

Hearing "Jingle Bells" in a store or watching children sleigh riding in their yards was so normal; it was surreal. Our world had changed so drastically; seeing others carry on as they always had made it feel almost as if Erin's death hadn't happened.

Only it had.

I struggled to smile because it hurt so deeply, and I felt slightly ashamed doing so. I felt guilty for smiling while Erin was dead and buried in the cold ground less than a mile away. I felt guilty for ruining everyone's holiday by being sad. I lost sight of the cheer in every image. Big parties and joyous celebrations rang on around me, but without Erin, I no longer felt I fit in with our "couple" friends, although they would insist otherwise. As my mental condition was questionable, my physical condition worsened.

I knew real adversity and perceived failure were gateways to my learning, but with every challenge this new existence offered came a plethora of loose ends, all inciting confrontation. Within the cross-examination between my own positive and negative thoughts, I knew I must somehow find a way to achieve peace.

In these days after losing Erin, I had been so focused on my personal failures and flaws that I had begun to overlook those things that were most important to remember, things like seeing the "J" in my name written as a heart by my girl, letting me know she loved me, or the priceless expressions on my children's faces as they read the loving words written to them by their mother. These simple yet powerfully important things would keep my darkness at bay. These simple things were the most important things, and I couldn't let them slip by me.

My walls had tumbled down around me. I had once lain there, pinned under the rubble, bitter and despondent. But it was now time to let these open wounds begin to heal. I could spend a lifetime playing the victim and easily adapt to this new way of life. I was an easy mark as I fell prey to scarlet tears that pierced this target upon my heart. Deep down inside lurked a sad clown, the nonconformist joker, a casualty of my own misguided perceptions. Was there no escaping this duress? I was grievously unschooled with the concept of loss.

I was angry. I knew in time my scars would fade, but I would never forget how they appeared. I must release this anger, or others would get hurt. Tantrum after tantrum had caused bitter turmoil inside as my inability to cope with anger in a healthy way had lent itself to this vicious, desperate cycle. I'd never seen another man so unstrung.

Back to that baseball toss out of the park and my ensuing tirade. *You stupid idiot. You stupid idiot!* Those were the words I said to myself over and over. Where did that shameful display come from? How did I reconcile my mishap? I did something that was seen by others as superhuman, and I received commendations, praise, and acclaim. In the recesses of my own mind, I was indicted, like a prisoner on trial.

Here we go again, slipping back into self-berating darkness.

I represented the prosecution. I was the judge, jury, and executioner. Was I guilty by reason of insanity? I could not live eternally with a lost soul within this fine line between madness and clarity. I was culpable among my peers, but, oblivious to the effects of my actions, and I never showed remorse. All these I confessed to Him now. I was a youthful offender, but I swear to tell the truth, the whole truth, and nothing but the truth, so help me God. I sat in my self-imposed cell, a detainee held captive by my own true visions.

I've come so far. I've learned so much. I can't unlearn what I've learned, what He has shown me. I can't go back there to desolate darkness again. I won't.

I was free falling with my family on board. I was spiraling toward the end, and what did I see? I pictured that poorly wired, hyperactive, sick little boy. Had he offered me wisdom with insight beyond his years? It felt as if it was just moments before impact. From this desperate bottom, could I emerge from the wreckage unscathed? Would I see things more clearly after the darkness from billowing smoke rises?

I had always struggled with shortsightedness, but this was far beyond sight and sound. How solid was my mind? Because I hadn't taken notice of my emotional challenges or dealt with them earlier on in my life, I was now forced to process all of it at once. My system was on overload my mind was short-circuiting, and it felt as if it would soon implode.

Where did all this internal commotion originate from? This was more than grief. I considered briefly the idea it might be born of hatred. I scrambled to answer.

I don't hate myself. Hate was such a despicable word. I decided it wasn't a matter of liking or hating but more about understanding and accepting myself. To do this, I knew I must respect myself, learn to want the best for myself, and I must commit to self-awareness and development.

I had been viewing my new world through a lens of loneliness and abandonment, and I now recognized my own child-like, self-absorbed reactions. I had to fully comprehend and accept that I had three young people, my children, who were counting on me to be strong and to guide them. Erin had lived, and we loved, and all of this havoc stemmed from a single, solitary, earth-shattering moment when the love of my life passed on.

My shock and grief had overwhelmed me with such brutality that I had no room for compassion. I pushed people away, offended that I was expected to still care about others while I was suffering. This reactive state of self-absorption bred isolation, and if I chose to go it alone, I would become that cold stone, easily tossed away, skipping across the surface before sinking alone to the dark, murky bottom.

Erin had once helped me to understand that not caring, not having compassion or empathy was a serious flaw in character. The way she cared for and stood by the people in her life spoke volumes about her character and had inspired me early on in our relationship to reevaluate my own. The example she set in her own life made me want to be a better person. When Erin passed away, that inspiration went with her. My caring left with her.

Caring hurts. It's why I'm hurting now. If I hadn't cared about Erin so much, this wouldn't be as painful.

For me, caring had always required the use of physical senses. When I lost Erin, I lost my way and with it my senses. I no longer saw her, so I had no desire to see. Life had lost its beauty. I couldn't hear her, so I no longer listened. I no longer cared what people had to say. None of it mattered to me. I couldn't taste her; therefore I became bitter. I no longer had a taste for living. I could no longer touch her, so why couldn't I let go?

I moved through the days following her death without sensitivity because I had lost the ability to care. Life seemed senseless because I had begun making it so. Now I was actively seeking out those sensations that I once knew. At times I wondered if I had lost them forever. I was still wrapped in self-consumption, but I had to break free, and allowing myself to care again was my only recourse.

The one I loved more than myself had died at my hands. This painful disease was literally devouring me, draining me of my strength, an ominous daily reminder that I am not well and that my own time might be limited.

Am I sure I don't hate myself? I destroyed my own true love, and now I'm destroying myself. Allowing myself to be consumed by hate and darkness would cause me to die even faster.

My children need me.

"God, please guide me through this."

Chapter 13

Faith Unwavered

I WAS SLAMMED WITH yet another powerful relapse of my disease, and outfitting myself with an appropriate emotion was inconceivable as they all seemed unsuitable. I was physically vulnerable at this point, and staying on track with my daily responsibilities was nearly impossible. The children's lives didn't go on hold just because I couldn't keep up, so I pushed myself to get through each day.

I still got up and corralled them off to school. They still needed lunches and rides to activities and their dad. They needed so much, and I felt like I had so little to give. Yet I pushed. *They need me.*

Once again, I could barely walk, and I needed Erin's strength now, perhaps more than ever. I appeared outwardly sickly, and comments like "Gosh, don't lose any more weight!" made by well-meaning neighbors and local parents confirmed it. Unfortunately, my polymyositis dictated for me how much weight I would retain or lose. Depending on the severity of the flare, as it is called, I could lose muscle at an alarming rate. Yanking on my belt tightly to the very last hole was my painful reminder of the stranglehold this disease had on me.

I was frightened. No, I was terrified. The symptoms had all returned in full force. This time, though, the onset was faster and more powerful like a steam engine that I had no idea how to operate. All my joints felt tender and hot to the touch. I was frail. I was frightened this could be it. I might not bounce back from this one.

My team of doctors turned to powerful pills and intravenous medicines to keep my body functioning, but the side effects of these toxic cocktails seemed to do more harm than good. It became difficult to tell if I was suffering from symptoms of the disease or from side effects from the treatment of the disease. Like a pit of quicksand that lacked surety, I feared eventually I would just fade away.

I tried various treatments and diet changes, including a holistic approach. I even went so far as to have the metal fillings removed from my mouth, thus eliminating any contaminants that might be triggering my immune system to destroy my own healthy tissues. It was all just stabbing blindly into the dark. No one really knew how to control this disease.

The more fragile I became emotionally and physically, the more isolated I felt. I didn't feel like there was anyone who could relate to me or who would *want* to. Creeping ever so slowly, thoughts of loneliness lovingly latched onto me. Suffocating from alienation and seclusion, consumed with my woes, I became a recluse facing extinction, this wasteland that offered no safe harbor. *I need Him.*

"God, please continue to guide me."

A frigid, cold winter made for a strong chill in the air. The last thing I wanted to do was venture out into it. Parental duties called, however. Kylie needed a ride home from her friend's house, and they were both sleeping at our house. I tiptoed carefully out the back door and saw the moonlight glistening off piles of snow all around me, wishing I could enjoy the beauty. Instead they symbolized the mountains that I couldn't climb. I backed the car out slowly and made my way to my daughter.

Kylie and Abby came bouncing out to the car laughing and talking. This was one of many sleepovers. Kylie was a social butterfly just like her mom.

"There they are!" I forced myself to smile. "Hi, girls!"

"Hi, Mr. Whit!" Abby called as she pulled open the rear car door. I felt a rush of frigid air enter the car and shuddered.

"Careful on that ice," I cautioned. "It's slippery!" Abby tossed her overnight bag into the back seat and climbed in. Kylie climbed in next to her in the back and hung over the front seat, adjusting the radio to her favorite station before plopping back in her seat. I slowly backed out of Abby's driveway and cautiously drove home, senses on high alert for black ice. Our driveway, of course, was a bit slick in spots, so I inched in carefully.

I was tired and ragged. It felt as if I was always running to catch up with my children and not doing a very good job. As the car slowly came to a stop, the girls opened their doors and climbed out.

For a split second, I was distracted as I opened my car door and began to step out. Caught off guard by the icy surface, the leg I extended slid forward, pulling me from my vehicle. I fell so quickly; there wasn't even time to panic. Hitting the ground, I bounced from its surface and, with a sharp jolt of pain, landed hard on the pavement with a sickening thud and an emptying breath.

Stunned, I could do nothing but lay where I landed in fetal position, cheek pressed numbingly on the frozen pavement, feeling helpless and beaten again.

"Dad, are you okay?" Kylie and Abby were peering down at me, stunned. My first thought was that I broke something. I took a quick inventory of my body, expecting to feel the evidence of serious damage. Thankfully, there was nothing immediately apparent.

I squirmed in the snow, attempting to roll over but in vain. My mind instantly flashed to Erin's lifeless body jumping up from the floor, but this time, I was the one shocked into submission.

I grew more concerned with each passing second in the cold as my weak body failed to right itself. My numb hands clawed for traction on the frozen surface below me, but I couldn't get a grip on anything useful to help me. I'd been here before—battered, helpless, limited.

"Kylie, please go get Brittany so you guys can help me up!" I gasped. The two girls turned and walked carefully to the house.

I tried again to pull myself up but to no avail. Lying upon the earth, frozen in time, feeling forsaken in the dark, bitter cold of the night, my troubles seemed amplified. My mind again flashed back to Erin lying on the floor, unresponsive, and panic began to build inside me. I struggled to summon enough strength in my arms and in my core to at least get myself up to my knees. I once again failed and sank back to the ground. I was humiliated and broken.

Am I not worthy?

My body began to tremble violently in reaction to the frigid cold. I was unable to tolerate the cold for more than a minute to two, or my breathing would become compromised. This scene had already been playing out too long, and it was not going to be good if I stayed here much longer. My teeth clashed against each other, and I tried to clench them together to prevent the chattering.

Please help me. As I lay there waiting for help to arrive, I felt a quiet glimmer of warm hope growing within. I knew it was my answer. I was going to be lifted from my situation very soon.

It will be okay. The girls are coming, and they will be able to help me up.

It occurred to me that if I had been alone here, had my daughter not been with me to see me fall, I could have quite possibly died in this very spot frozen. No one would know I was here, and I couldn't reach my phone. Within a few minutes, I would be so cold. I would not even be able to breathe well enough to yell out for help.

Erin's fate had been realized. She was not to be revived. She was to be exalted and revered. I was to be helped up and revived. Yes, I was lying here, much like Erin had been that night—helpless. Unlike Erin, I was given the precious chance to live. I knew from this moment on that I must appreciate the opportunity I had been afforded. It must not be wasted.

I am worthy.

I waited patiently, and soon my girls came sliding over to me.

"Dad! What happened?" Brittany cried out, leaning down to see me better. "Are you okay?"

"I will be. Together," I said, "we can get this done." She and Kylie nodded in unison, worried but determined.

I instructed each of them to take an arm and help me to my knees. They struggled with my weight and awkwardness but managed to hoist me up. It felt good to be up off the snow and ice. I told them each to grab an arm and warned them they must be strong so I could make it to my feet. My legs were not strong enough to push me up on their own.

I counted, "One, two, three," and shouted at them to lift me. Halfway through, I cried louder, "Stronger, girls, we're almost there!" My little girls somehow found the strength to lift my 150 pounds of deadweight until I managed to extend my legs just far enough to help them the rest of the way.

It was a huge relief to stand once again on my own two feet, such a simple task that I couldn't have accomplished without my children.

Thank you.

CHAPTER 14

CONFIRMATION

I STOOD IN MY marble shower and let the hot water run over my aching body. The heat soothed my physical pain but didn't soak in deep enough to touch my emotional wounds. I wondered how much longer I could do this, not out of self-pity but practical curiosity. How much longer would my eroding body be able to withstand the assault it was waging on itself? It would have to give out at some point. When?

The disease had spread to my lungs, causing scarring and compromised breathing. This was a game changer and could result in a much shorter life for me. I thought of my children, and my heart ached. How would they be able to withstand the loss of *both* parents? I had life insurance and had carefully drawn up a will. I was very proactive with regard to securing their futures financially but emotionally? I covered my face with one hand. I just couldn't imagine.

Why? Why must we continue to be tortured like this?

As had now become a familiar routine, I began peeling off the tattered Band-Aids that I wore on my fingertips to protect the cracked and bleeding skin underneath. Every fingertip and all around my fingernails were covered with angry, open fissures, some up to an inch in length that were excruciatingly painful to the touch and bled profusely. Mechanic's hands it was called. It was yet another fun symptom of this disease.

I slowly poured the shampoo into my palm and reached up to lather my hair. I felt the familiar burning and trembling of my shoulders as they strained to lift my arms up. This was followed by searing pain across my fingers as the shampoo seeped into the open cracks in the skin, adding insult to injury. I quickly ran my stinging fingers under the water to rinse the harsh soap out. As the pain eased in my hands, I tilted my head back under the water and closed my eyes.

Ridiculous. The simplest of tasks becomes torture.

As the hot water and lather slipped over my emaciated frame, I looked down at my once athletic legs, barely recognizable now. I held my arm out in front of me and took in the protruding wrist bones and elbows. Erin's favorite feature of mine had always been my muscular arms. Like Erin, they, too, were no more. I looked at the random bruises scattered over my body. Corticosteroids were wreaking havoc on me yet somehow keeping me alive. I even had bruises on my hip bones where the waistband of my underwear rested on my skin.

I'm so fragile now.

I could feel it all well up inside me, all of it. I was trying hard to keep it together and under control. I was doing the work emotionally and spiritually, and just as I was beginning to really start making progress, my body started to fail me. Again.

I'm trying my best, and it just keeps getting harder.

I didn't feel the tears because they simply spilled from my eyes and merged with the hot water of the shower, but I knew they were there. This time I succumbed to them and let them carry me away. I began to weep. The sobs wracked my stricken body as all of the pent-up grief, the unspoken words, the smothered cries of pain, fear, loneliness, and shame came pouring out of me in torrents and were washed away, swirling down the drain.

I cried for the little boy who couldn't control his body or his thoughts. I cried for the man he grew into, whose body was now controlling him. I cried for my beautiful girl who didn't get to live to see her children grow, and I cried for my children who someday soon might not have parents to guide them. I cried until I simply could not cry anymore and until the hot water began to cool.

Finally exhausted, I opened the glass door of the shower, stepped out into the cool air of the bathroom. I stepped slowly and very carefully across the gray marble floor. As I reached the vanity, I placed both hands on the counter to support my unformidable upper body. My eyes were cast downward. Erin had been so strong, and I was now dying for that strength literally.

"I am doing everything You asked. How much more am I supposed to take from You?" I looked up and saw my face in the mirror, eyes swollen from crying. I saw a little boy in a man's broken body. "I'm not strong enough to keep doing this." My eyes traveled to another reflection in the mirror. It was a clear reflection of the rear view of me in the glass shower door that hung behind me.

The bright sunlight from the bathroom window streamed across my back, and what I saw in that reflection was a stark contrast to the person I had just seen in front of me. This was the back of a man. The sun highlighted the contours of muscle in my broad upper back and shoulders. They looked strong, stronger than they felt.

This was him.

CHAPTER 15

FEEL THROUGH ME

I HAD ALWAYS HATED moving slowly. I couldn't do it. The twenty-five speeding tickets I had amassed over my adult life attested to that. I had always associated moving slowly with restriction and hardship.

Managing time had never come easily to me. It had always seemed to pass right through me undetected. I lost track of time constantly. I was always running late or missing deadlines. My illness demanded that I move slowly and methodically, and I soon discovered I actually felt more control. I started taking time to ponder decisions and weigh them out before acting because movement was so painful and difficult. To reduce my suffering, I had to become more proactive and less reactive.

Each new day brought with it the same old, unrelenting physical pain, and the medications being offered were doing little to relieve it. In fact, my latest round of pills seemed to have accelerated my dissent.

As much as I longed for the hurting to stop, I was not yet ready to face my own imminent flatline, which at this point seemed to be the only possible relief from the pain. I was slowly but surely withering away. If I couldn't somehow get the effects of this insidious disease under control, I feared I might not have much time left at all.

I knew my body well. Indeed, my latest blood work indicated my CK level was once again at dangerously high levels. This test measured the amount of active inflammation in the body. The normal level for this marker is between 50 and 160. Mine was now reading 11,000. Just as I had suspected, the inflammation was running rampant, and my muscles were being destroyed at a higher rate of speed. I had lost twelve pounds in one month. Already underweight, I now looked frighteningly thin as I was being force-fed to death.

I regretted not taking better care of myself. Don't we all at some point in our lives? Looking back over the years, it was clear that I made a habit of working harder, not smarter. What was it my teacher had said? "He functions best when he has twice as much to do as the other children, but this is not always possible." That trait had carried over into my adult years where I hadn't felt comfortable if I didn't have at least ten projects going on at the same time.

It was no wonder my body finally rebelled. I ran myself right into the ground, working a full-time job, maintaining our twenty investment apartments, staying up all hours of the night renovating our own house. This was all normal for me. Perhaps I had been fueling my drive to succeed with my pent-up anger and frustration from earlier years, reconfiguring it for a more positive outcome. Perhaps I was trying to use my energy for something good instead of evil.

At what cost?

I knew I had not finished my work here in this physical world yet. I knew there was more He wanted me to accomplish. I now worked feverishly to learn about the meaning and purpose of my life and how it impacted others. I feared my time here might be running out. How would it end? Would I just continue living and suffering with this nasty condition, the quality of my life diminishing with my body until there was nothing left? Or would the end of the line come quickly, maybe suddenly, like I knew all too well it could?

What would I leave behind as my legacy, my imprint on this world? Would it be a positive one? Even if we'd directly impacted only one other life on this earth, we'd left a mark, a trace that we once existed. I wanted mine to be a positive one.

I began to think of each of our lives being like that smooth stone cast out across the surface of the water, skipping until finally disappearing. The ripples it left behind continued to spread across the water long after the stone was gone. This was how I imagined our presence on this earth. I thought of Erin and all the wonderful ripples she had sent out into the world. They were still spreading, even after she was gone. Every time one of her children smiled or one of her friends was inspired to do something kind for another, as Erin had so often done—these were ripples that were started by Erin's presence in this world. Perhaps they were part of the meaning and purpose of her life; perhaps they *were* her eternal life.

While we are among the living, it seems our ripples or messages or life's purpose may not be as impactful as they are after we pass. Perhaps in dying, our lives take on their fullest meaning.

This was the sense of urgency I was feeling as I prepared for the end of my life, clashing with the elements of my past. I knew for me to leave a positive imprint on this world, I would have to leave my troubles behind and truly see myself through His eyes. I would need to feel the truth of myself through Him. Through this, I must find eternal peace.

Please guide me.

CHAPTER 16

TILL DEATH DO US PART

I DREAMED OF ERIN, and I found her. I longed for a deep connection with someone, someone I could share my life with and breathe together with in unison for a lifetime. I knew it was going to take a very special person to understand me and love me the way I needed to be loved. I was not easy to love with all my complicated wiring, whirling thoughts and emotions. Whoever this fantasy woman was, she would have to have a strong sense of self and be just dynamic enough to keep me focused so I could love her the way she needed to be loved. All of this had to be reciprocal, or it would never last. That was a tall order, and I seriously questioned if I would ever find that girl.

And then she hit me in the eye with an orange, and I knew I had found her. As I wiped the orange juice from my stinging eye, I *knew*.

Erin had so instantly captivated me on every level. I needed to know if this girl could have possibly been real. A touch confirmed it, and from that moment on, I dreamt about being with her, spending all of our days together living as one in a never-ending embrace. As it turned out, we *had* breathed together in unison for a lifetime; the lifetime turned out to be much shorter than either of us had imagined. It was a breath that almost saved her, as her breath had saved me.

Sharing a life with Erin had helped transform me into a better person. She helped me to appreciate and focus on the here and now and gave new value to my precious time. She had a very clear vision of life and how it should be lived, and all of it felt possible as long as she was near. Erin touched all things in me and made them better.

And then she was gone. Her sudden disappearance had left me feeling shell-shocked and disoriented. It had all happened so suddenly; there were moments I wondered if she had even existed at all. I was left with an inability to let go and move on. I stopped thriving. I blamed myself, and I couldn't find peace.

Broken and left to find my way without my other half, I had grown to understand the importance of seeing life clearly for myself. I discovered that I was stronger than I had ever imagined, and perhaps because Erin was no longer able to, I began to appreciate the simple blessings in life again. Through her sudden departure, Erin was once more helping me to be strong and to evolve. It was her final gift to me and perhaps her most important.

The pain of losing Erin had so broken me, it was devastating enough to bring me back to my faith, back to Him. Through Him, I began to understand that there were reasons for events in our lives that we might not understand right away, if ever. He knows the deeper meaning of all things, and if we are open and willing, He will show us.

I sought to find peace by transforming myself into a better person. I began to see myself through His eyes, the loving and compassionate eyes of a parent. I began to recognize Him in myself and everyone around me. My vivid dream in which Erin and I held each other and spoke without words showed me the part of Him that had lived within Erin as well. That warm light she emanated, the special way she made us all feel when we were near her—she had *always* seen me through His eyes.

Erin's love had illuminated a path I hadn't realized I was meant to follow on my own—the path to Him and eternal peace.

Now I knew it was time to say goodbye to my true love, my girl. I had been terrified to let her go, out of fear of erasing all memories of her. I feared they would disappear as suddenly as she had. In the days since Erin passed, I had learned that the memories I had of her were all right there, tucked away safe in my heart where they would always remain. The light and love that Erin brought into this world did not die with her. I had the honor of witnessing it every day as I continued raising our three beautiful children, created out of our love for each other. Her love and light indeed shone on.

The truth was, she was never mine. I was blessed to have been the one chosen to walk alongside her for the rest of her days, to share dreams with, to grow with, to laugh with and cry with. *Till death do us part.* Erin and I had fulfilled every one of our marriage vows to each other. "I agree to have and to hold you from this day forward, to honor and to cherish, for richer or poorer, for better or worse, in sickness and in health, till death do us part."

I had loved her deeply as she did me until death and forever after, but I had to finally accept that the time for us to live in this world together had now come and gone, and it was time to set her free. It was time to set myself free.

I loved the things I saw in you, Erin. I honored all the ways in which you touched me, and I'll cherish the way you feel through me forever. So I stand now and back away, and I relinquish your final breath to Him and ensure deliverance to the One who gave it, setting free two birds to fly from the edge with hurling force and the rolling sound of one grounded stone bearing my name, claiming your rightful place in heaven, the place where there is no death and dying, no mourning and no pain.

CHAPTER 17

LIVING THE WORD

CLANK! CLANK! CLANK! CLANK!

The wheels of the gurney hit each stair with a heavy jolt, and although I was securely strapped in, my body lurched with each intense impact. The EMTs were moving quickly. Activity swirled around me like a tornado—the clanking of equipment, staticky, muffled sounds of the officers' radios, loud footsteps on the stairs. The scene was eerily familiar, and it was not one I wanted to participate in again. Yet, here I was.

"John, I'm coming with you!" my sister Laura called out to me as I was wheeled past her and out the back door to the awaiting ambulance. I looked up to see Brittany, Kylie, and Johnny looking down from the second-floor window, faces pale with fear. I shook my head ever so slightly. I had told Brittany specifically to not look out the window this time. I couldn't imagine the trauma she was reliving, having already watched the nearly identical scene with her mother several years earlier; her mother never came home. She later wrote in a school paper that her mother's face "was as white as the snow."

Once inside the ambulance, the paramedic put an oxygen mask over my face and immediately began checking my vitals.

"Just relax now, okay? We'll be at the hospital soon."

With every bump in the road, the contents of the ambulance heaved and rattled, me included. The EMT was unfazed and went about the business of examining me.

Over the past couple of weeks, I had been growing weaker at an alarming rate of speed, and my usually sporadic dry cough had become constant, deeper, and unproductive.

My sister Susan, a nurse practitioner, pleaded with me to go the hospital several times from her home in Cape Cod, about three hours away.

"I don't think it's that serious," I lied into the phone. "Let's give it a bit more time. Maybe I'll start to feel better." The truth was, I was afraid. I didn't want to hear what the doctors had to say.

Eighteen months earlier at one of my many doctor's visits, I had been diagnosed with pulmonary fibrosis, a progressive scarring of the lungs caused by the inflammation that was eating away at the rest of me. As with my polymyositis, there was no cure. This new complication was life-threatening and was a leading cause of death for patients with this illness.

"What's the worst-case scenario for this? How much time do I have?" I had asked. My doctor was stone-faced.

"Worst case? Eighteen to twenty-four months. But people can live for twenty years or more. There's really no telling."

That was eighteen months ago. This is it.

For the past few days, as long as I sat still and didn't move, I was fine, except for the hacking, violent cough. If I stood up or attempted to walk, I couldn't breathe, and I grew dizzy. So I didn't stand up unless it was absolutely necessary. My kids became extensions of me. I called to them from the couch and gave them instructions.

"Kylie, let the dogs out and make sure they go. Stand there for at least fifteen minutes. Don't let them in unless they go."

"Johnny, can you bring me my pills and some water?"

Britt, my little motherly daughter, stepped right up and made sure I ate and that her siblings were helping. This was how we functioned.

One morning, I woke up struggling to breathe, even while sitting or lying down. I couldn't catch my breath between spastic coughing fits. Dea, always there for us during health crises, came to the house and tested my oxygen levels. Not good. That would explain the blue tinge to my extremities. We were all thinking the same thing; the lung disease was progressing.

Not satisfied with the fragmented updates she was receiving, Susan came down from Cape Cod to see me for herself.

"Oh my god, John," she said, breezing into the living room. "You look awful." She tossed her coat onto a chair and placed a hand on my forehead. "You're burning up." She shook her head, lips pursed together. She looked worried. After a quick check of the vitals, she looked at me sternly. "We are getting you to the hospital now." All I could do was nod in agreement. With much effort, she and the kids got me into the back seat of her car, and we sped off toward the hospital.

Susan rounded up a wheelchair for me and quickly wheeled me into the emergency room, right up to the admitting desk. Because of her credentials and knowing what to say, she was able to get me into a room very quickly.

My sister Susan was also my health-care proxy and the executor of my will. She came well prepared with all the pertinent documents. When she informed me that she had brought them, the grave reality began to seep in. *My kids.*

The doctor was standing and typing my information into the computer next to my bed.

"Mr. Whitmeyer, it says here you have signed a DNR, a Do Not Resuscitate order. Is that right? You do not want to be resuscitated?"

"I did?" I was startled.

"Yes, John, you had it written into your will, remember?" Susan answered softly. It hit me hard. When I had my will drawn up sometime ago, I was freshly reeling from Erin's death and hadn't wanted to be revived. It sounded so harsh now. *My kids.*

"Mr. Whitmeyer, do you want to change it?" The doctor had turned from the computer to fix his gaze on me.

"Well, what does resuscitate mean exactly?"

"If you should go into cardiac arrest, do you want to have CPR performed?"

"Yes."

"If you are unable to breathe on your own, do you want to be ventilated/intubated?"

"You mean a breathing tube?" I balked. "I don't want a breathing tube."

"What if the breathing tube was a temporary measure?" Susan asked.

"Oh well, yeah!" I replied. "If it's temporary, sure, but if it's not ever coming out, then no." The doctor typed the changes into the computer. "If there is a chance I will recover, I want to be resuscitated. If I'm not able to function independently, then don't resuscitate me."

This conversation brought to light a harsh reality I had not wanted to fully accept. My children could very easily be parentless in the near future, orphans.

My God. Both parents dead. Was this really part of His plan?

I couldn't imagine that it was. They had been through enough already.

The doctor stepped away from the computer and stood at the foot of the bed.

"We are going to run some more tests, get a scan done of your lungs, and get a better feel for what we are dealing with here, okay? We're going to get you admitted to a room, at least for tonight."

"Sounds good," I said weakly, although it sounded anything but that.

My kids must be so worried. I needed to get home to them as soon as possible.

The next day, after tests and examinations and horrible hospital food, the doctor finally returned to my room.

"Well, it appears the lung disease has progressed very minimally. In fact, some areas show improvement over your last scan. We can't find anything significant. It appears to be viral." Relieved, Susan and I sighed in unison.

"We are going to send you home because quite honestly, you are safer there than you are here. If we keep you here in this environment, the chances of you picking up something like pneumonia are much higher, and in your present state, that would be very dangerous. So go home, rest, drink plenty of fluids, and let this thing run its course."

As the relief washed over me, replacing my cold fear, I thanked him. I was going home to my kids. Tears sprang to my eyes, but for the first time in a very long time, they were tears of joy and appreciation. I thanked Him as well.

Arriving home, we were met with plenty of hugs and smiles and exclamations of joy. My heart was full. My sister Laura came down for the week to help care for me and to start me on a new anti-inflammatory diet that had helped relieve her MS symptoms. The house was bustling with activity, and I dedicated myself to following the doctor's and Laura's orders so I could get back to the gift of living a full life.

The annoying, disruptive cough continued, and my weakness persisted, but I was determined to beat this thing. I had a lot of things to get to.

Lying on the couch for days on end gave me plenty of time to think. My thoughts were consumed with the kids, how they were feeling about my close call and about their futures.

I needed to talk with them, hear them out, and let them know what the plan was, should something happen to me. I was fortunate enough to return home from the hospital this time, but at some point in the near future, we might not be as blessed. I wanted to take this opportunity I had been given and reassure them that there were plans in place to make sure they were well cared for, should something go terribly wrong. They wouldn't be left on their own to find their way in the world.

One morning I corralled them all into the living room, announcing I wanted to talk with them.

"What's up, fella?" Johnny asked, plopping down in chair. I looked at his long body stretched across the chair. Entering adolescence now, Johnny was beginning to look like a young man. Time seemed to be passing more quickly, and I felt a sense of urgency to ensure my kids' futures were well-planned for.

"Well, I wanted to talk with you about some important stuff. I know you must have been really worried while I was in the hospital." All three sets of eyes were glued on me as I spoke.

"Yeah, well, when Mommy went to the hospital, she didn't come home, so…" Kylie's voice trailed off.

"I know, honey. That's why I wanted to talk with you, guys. I want to hear how you are feeling. What kinds of things are you thinking about?" I began coughing, and it carried on for quite a while.

"If you die, where will we live? Will we go live with Aunt Sue?" Kylie quickly asked.

"Kylie!" Brittany exclaimed, offended. "That's a terrible thing to say!"

"No, it's okay, Britt. It's a good question and an important one," I replied, finally recovering from the coughing fit.

And so the extremely difficult yet imperative conversation began. As I explained the game plan to my children, I could see their relief growing, mixing with sadness, confusion, and anger. Oddly, I felt stronger in that moment than I had in a very long time. I knew what my kids needed, and I was giving it to them. No one wants to talk about this stuff, but I knew it would help them in the long run. Certainty quells fear.

And now here I was days later, speeding toward the hospital in the back of an ambulance with the events of the afternoon replaying in my mind. I had collapsed in the shower, unable to breathe. I somehow staggered, dripping and cold to the chair in my bedroom; where I continued to gasp frantically for air. Coughing uncontrollably, I grabbed wildly for a blanket, pulled it off the bed, and covered myself. By the time Brittany and my sister Laura found me, I had turned blue.

"Oh my god! What happened?" Laura ran over to me. "Britt, come help me get him to the bed!"

Once in bed and wrapped in blankets and comforters, my body temperature began to regulate, but I was still gasping for air, and the body-wracking cough was nonstop.

"We need to get you to the hospital, John. There's no question now." Laura and the kids hovered nervously over me. Too weak to put up any kind of resistance, I conceded.

Moments later in an improbable twist of fate, my quiet bedroom was once again filled with bustling EMTs, strange medical equipment, and police officers. I heard the familiar beeping of an ambulance backing up to the door, and I realized I was lying in the exact spot Erin had been lying in the last time this scene played out in our room.

As the ambulance pulled into the hospital parking lot, I was hauled out of the back and quickly wheeled right into a well-lit room in triage, filled with nurses and doctors poised for action. They quickly transferred me from the gurney to the awaiting bed and sprang into well-organized action. It was an amazing sight to behold, this group of people working together seamlessly. It was like watching an efficiently designed machine.

Countless tests were performed. They even had an X-ray machine set up in the room, and they were able to take scans of my chest right there on the spot. Laura had followed the ambulance and was sitting in the room with me when the doctor returned about an hour later.

I was exhausted and relieved to be under warm blankets and in the care of professionals. I knew I was where I needed to be and felt an oddly out-of-place sense of calm. I contemplated the idea that I once again found myself of the precipice between life and death, and yet I was feeling very different about it this time. In a spiritual sense, I felt more prepared to face the afterlife, yet in more earthly ways, I was not. I wasn't ready to leave my children. They were too young, and they had already been through so much.

No, not ready to leave this life yet. My kids need me.

"I want to give you a preliminary update. We are still waiting on some results, but we have been able to rule out a number of things. The lung disease has not progressed. We suspect you have an upper respiratory infection and are going to admit you into step-down ICU and start you on strong antibiotics while we wait for more test results. We want to rule out the possibility of pneumonia."

He was very matter-of-fact, and as he spoke, I felt reassured. Laura and I exchanged quick glances. An upper respiratory infection seemed very manageable, although the step-down ICU sounded a bit ominous. I was only one step away from being in the intensive care unit.

The tests for pneumonia came back negative, so I was transferred out of step-down ICU into a regular room where I remained for several more days, improving all the while. The antibiotics were working.

Over the course of my time there, it became obvious that my lack of mobility for such an extended period of time was having a cumulative effect. I was released to an inpatient rehabilitation center where I would continue my recovery and regain my strength so I could resume life on my own again.

I was fortunate that the Gaylord Rehabilitation Center had an available room for me. They came highly recommended for their outstanding care and success rate. Over the next four weeks, my days were packed tightly with structured therapies—pulmonary therapy to help improve my breathing and stamina, physical therapy to strengthen targeted muscle groups, and occupational therapy to strengthen the muscles associated with day-to-day activities. In between, there was rest and highly nutritious meals. I had lost a lot of weight over the previous couple of weeks, and the focus was on caloric intake and lots of protein.

The sessions were grueling. I was unable to move about on my own, so we really had to start with basic fundamentals. Because I was not strong enough to walk safely on my own, there was an alarm on my bed that signaled the staff if I got up and tried to walk without someone there to assist.

The staff were friendly and supportive, and I began forming bonds with them right away. Apparently, word had gotten out among my friends that I had been in the hospital, and I had visitors stopping by regularly to see how I was doing, usually bringing pizza and other goodies with them. These visits lifted my spirits and inspired me to work that much harder to heal and recover my independence.

My sessions in the large gym became highly motivating for me. I was seeing my own progress as well as the progress of others around me. My eyes had always been drawn to movement, and in the large gym, there was a lot of movement and all different people in various states of disability. I was fascinated on a daily basis. I took it all in with a curious mind. I wanted to know all their stories, including the staff.

Many of the patients appeared in far worse condition than mine, and I was grateful for the chance to make a full recovery, as I realized some of us did not have the same opportunity. There was a sense of comradery among the patients. We all understood how it felt to be weak and have daunting tasks ahead of us.

I became friendly with a man who I noticed had a similar schedule to mine. We were often in the gym at the same time. Dave was about my age, and one of his legs had recently been amputated from above the knee.

"What are you in for?" I asked as the nurse parked my wheelchair next to his. This was a common question among patients.

"Ah, I have diabetes and had my leg cut off, just trying to get back on my foot." We both laughed. "How about you?" My story didn't sound nearly as dramatic as his.

"Well, I don't think I can compete with *that* one. I just have a muscle disease and got a chest infection. It nearly did me in." He nodded. It didn't really matter why we were there; the fact that we were was unifying enough. It was an environment where we all felt comfortable answering such questions honestly, without fear of boring the other person or sounding like a downer. There was an unspoken understanding between most of us.

As time passed and I began to make progress in my recovery, I noticed the other patients and their progress. I looked around the large gym one morning and as usual, took in the sights and sounds of the other patients working hard, pushing themselves, at varying levels of ability. Their physical therapists looked on, offering words of encouragement and positive feedback. There was a certain energy present here. It was empowering and compassionate, inspiring and comforting, and it seemed to emanate from the staff as much as it did the patients.

"You've got this, Tom. You can do it! One more!" Tom was shaking with effort as he stepped slowly, one unsure foot at a time, supporting himself with his upper body as he made his way down the length of the twenty-foot parallel bars. I was glued, watching to see how far he would make it this time. I had seen him make it to about the halfway mark before but never farther.

Tom looked for a moment like he wanted to give up, and I saw him size up the distance to the end of the bars. I saw the expression of surrender on his face slowly change into one of determination and sheer will. Tom fixed his eyes on the ends of the bars and, with a bit more energy, stepped and pushed his way down the length of them to the end. When he reached his goal, his therapists and other patients who had been watching, including myself, all cheered. Tom smiled broadly, exhausted but proud.

My eyes drifted to a very thin woman sitting in a wheelchair, wearing a protective helmet. Her therapists carefully moved her to a padded physical-therapy table. As she sat there, it was obvious she had a number of major issues, some possibly neurological. She didn't seem completely coherent. The seriousness of her condition struck me.

Oh my gosh, she is having such a difficult time.

"God," I prayed, "please help her. Please give her the strength she is lacking."

I watched as her physical therapist kneeled down on the floor in front of her, looked directly into her eyes, and kept her engaged as he spoke. He seemed to be outlining for her what the next exercise would be, and I was taken with the exchange. I couldn't look away. The therapist had established a strong connection with his patient and was able to maintain it very effectively. This important connection was a crucial factor in his ability to help her do the work necessary for her recovery.

Not unlike the connection He makes with all of us, so we are able do the work necessary to help ourselves heal.

I suddenly saw Him clearly working in everyone around me. It became so apparent to me. I couldn't believe I hadn't seen it before. He was the source of the energy I sensed.

He works through every one of us. We are all here to help each other move in a direction towards Him and healing.

I felt a warmth and surety of knowledge I had never quite felt before. As I moved through my days, I began to see each person I encountered in a different light. I saw Him in every one of them, and once seen, I could not look at them with anything less than compassion, empathy, and appreciation.

Everyone has their own story. Their own journey to Him. Everyone's story is as important and unique as another's. We are all here doing the same good work, persevering through our own individual hardships and adversity so that we may know peace.

My epiphany was about so much more than physical recovery; it was about *spiritual recovery.* It was as if the physical world surrounding me was mirroring what was also happening on the spiritual level. Just as every patient had their own story about why they were here, so we all have our own spiritual story about discovering the purpose and meaning behind our lives. We all have work to do in order to heal. In turning away from it or denying it, we only prolong the suffering. If we trust in Him to guide us through our lessons, we will then be able to do the necessary work to heal our spirits.

One rainy afternoon, I was once again in the gym, throwing around the heavy brown medicine ball, my least favorite exercise. I looked up to see the woman from the other day wearing her helmet and being pushed in her wheelchair by a man, who might have been her husband.

As before, the therapists helped her move from her wheelchair to the low, padded table, and she sat down. This time, one of her therapists pushed a walker in front of her.

"We're going to try this today, okay?" They helped her up to a standing position and placed her hands on the walker. She looked very unsteady on her feet, and I was afraid this would not end well. The therapists guided her to take a step, and she did cautiously and with success. I breathed a sigh of relief.

Then to everyone's surprise, she took another step, followed by another and another, and before any of us knew what was happening, she was walking across the room almost effortlessly. Her therapists called out and ran after her.

"Whoah! Take it easy! Slow down. You don't want to go too fast!"

"Oh my gosh! I've never seen anything *like* that!" I heard one staff member exclaim. To all our amazement, the woman tried to ditch the walker, kicking it to the side with her foot, and proceeded to walk unaided. Her therapist was panicked and insisted she use the walker. It was hard to believe this was the same immobile woman I had seen the other day.

She walked right past me, and I almost fell over when she turned to me with a wink and a reassuring nod of her head, as if to say, "I got this!" I could only stare in amazement. I smiled and nodded back at her as if to say, "Yes, you do!"

I began to notice that people were approaching me more often, wanting to chat. They pulled up in their wheelchairs or sat down next to me, and we talked. One therapist opened up to me about her boyfriend, another talked with me about her mother. I loved listening to them talk. I loved hearing about their backgrounds, their colorful dreams, and their disappointments. As I listened, I picked up on little bits of wisdom and guidance that provided answers to questions I didn't realize I had. I could clearly see Him working through every one of them.

"John Whitmeyer!" said one night-shift nurse as she read my chart. "That sounds like an author's name! Do you write?" I stared at her for a split second, surprised.

"Well, I sort of just started writing," I replied, smiling. "I'll take that as a confirmation that I should keep doing it!"

"What are you writing?" she asked.

"I'm not quite sure yet. I have been keeping a journal since my wife passed away. It helps me sort things out."

"I'm so sorry to hear that. I'm glad something good is coming out of such a tragedy."

And so it was for the rest of my stay there; stories were shared, and bonds were formed. When I was discharged from the facility, one of the staff called out, "The Mayor of Gaylord is finally on his way home." I laughed and high-fived him. I had gone from a recluse facing my own extinction to The Mayor.

This was Him.

CHAPTER 18

REDEMPTION AT LAST

I PUSHED SOMEONE TO the ground, and I didn't like being disciplined. Others suffered from my actions, and I thought it was acceptable. I carelessly struck another with my stone, and there was applause. I ran from another in need, acting on my own fears. Consumed with internal shame, I felt it was rightly deserved. I lashed out in anger, only to inflict blind fury on those around me, and I emitted harmful resentment, questioning my faith.

I stumbled. I fell, and I couldn't get up, but it was from that ground I grew. Eternal peace begins and ends with Him in all His forms, including me. For most of my life, I thought having a full and happy life meant having someone to love, a nice, big house, tangible things to furnish it with, and enough money in the bank to have some fun. As it turned out, having a full and happy life for me was not about framing a bigger, stronger house; it was about recognizing Him in myself, in every situation I encountered, in every person I crossed paths with and being open to receiving the guidance He was offering through all of it. It was about reinforcing my inner self, my house, with a solid foundation, bearing the building blocks of constructive thoughts and emotions. These were not new concepts. I believed they had been described throughout time itself in different mediums, different languages, using different words and imagery to convey the same unifying truth. The answers lie within because He is within all of us.

This was what I recognized and loved in Erin. The very light and vibrant energy I loved in her and had come to depend on had been within me all along. I had grown blind to it, but she saw it clearly. And she loved me for it too. I was searching outside myself for something I already had within me. I just had to remember.

Loving Erin as deeply and powerfully as I did and then losing her as suddenly and traumatically as I did ripped me open to the core and brought me to my knees. Only the most powerful love was that devastating when it was lost, and it had to be that way, or I would never have been brought to the edge of madness and desolation, staring down my own in-between. Only by being completely broken was I made ready.

And then He touched me. He gave me a glimpse of something greater. Something I had lost along the way, something I had forgotten. My true self, as He saw me, through the eyes of a loving parent, that parent that I lacked. Three wise words rocketed through me in thought and now appeared as written words. They had aligned like literary stars lighting my way right to Him.

I traveled back to the beginning where I had made my first tragic mistake, the place where I could start to remove the original rubble that had fallen down, burying me. It was there in that classroom I began to really forget who I was, and my attention was drawn outward, away from Him and my true self. With each dark memory of past events, I could see where another layer of rubble had been added, making it harder and harder to remember who I really was.

As I found the courage to face each of these moments and understand the circumstances behind the events, the rubble began to loosen. It was frightening at first, uncovering myself. Looking at myself, the young boy, as something other than a flawed, poorly-wired problem child left me feeling exposed and vulnerable. I knew I must continue to do this good work. He was urging me on. I had judged myself. I had thrown words around like perfect stones. Some had returned to me, and I felt the sting as they struck me and knocked me down. Once I cast them out, I couldn't retrieve them. I could only act accordingly with sympathy and compassion. In these ways, I failed myself, yet now expected of myself to achieve something extraordinary, something superhuman. I couldn't allow self-doubt to impede my growth. Anger, guilt and shame just stood in the way of true change.

A keen sense guided me to recognize my own self-destructive nature, to understand it, and to lay myself bare for everyone to see. The results were surprising—the question of faith was answered with clarity, and my energy was refocused on my commitment to Him with confidence and certainty. I harnessed His spirit, allowing goodness to penetrate the broken walls of my fortress, and I accepted it to radiate openly through me. I had to harmonize so the defense could rest and build on this life in peace and not war.

The light was pouring into my life as I continued doing my good work. I began to view the world and people in it differently. I began to see the common threads connecting us all. Seemingly random and abstract events began to show patterns and symmetry. The world around me began to make sense. I could see the meaning and purpose in all things. I could see His hand in all our lives. This was Him.

My own two eyes adjusted like the lens of a camera, serving as my confessional. My pessimism called into question popular opinions, and wounded, I limped against the herd. What would my summation entail? I have presented the evidence, and I attested to this deposition after offering confirmation with my sworn oath. I threw caution to any story that held untruths. So I gave hard facts careful consideration. I am a credible witness you can all believe. I couldn't be just another fatality, forever fleeing from darkness. *God, please deliver me from evil. I can't follow, so I will lead. I was bitter, but I could savor. I can't touch, but I can feel.*

This is my testimony, but it is no submission for just one man. It is the story of one man's struggle, body over mind and mind over body, who finally found peace by surrendering both over to Him and the truth of the light.

"The Light shines in the darkness, and the darkness has not overcome it" (John 1:5).

"He came as a witness to testify concerning that light, so that through him all might believe" (John 1:7).

ABOUT THE AUTHOR

JOHN WHITMEYER WAS BORN in New Jersey and raised in a small town in Western Connecticut. He graduated from Southern Connecticut State University with a degree in social work. He has been writing for nine years while raising his three children. *Feel through Me* is his first memoir.

CPSIA information can be obtained
at www.ICGtesting.com
Printed in the USA
BVHW030147160919
558529BV00001B/52/P